Modelling the

LMSR

Chris Ellis

LONDON
IAN ALLAN LTD

MODELLING THE LMSR

Contents

First published 1985

ISBN 0 7110 1498 1

Published by Ian Allan Ltd, Shepperton, Surrey; and printed by Ian Allan Printing Ltd at their works at Coombelands in Runnymede, England

Cover

The LMSR atmosphere in 7mm scale, 0 gauge, as No 6110 *Grenadier Guardsman*, parallel boiler 'Royal Scot' class, heads a train of standard Stanier coaches out of Helmshore station on the layout of Hyndburn Model Railway Group. All the models are accurately lined out and painted as for the later 1930s period when chrome yellow replaced straw yellow in the lining, locomotive wheels were no longer lined out, and coach ends were black. *Brian Monaghan*

Far right:

The Midland Railway Fowler '4F' 0-6-0 design was continued in large numbers by the LMSR as a general-purpose class prior to the introduction of larger more modern designs. This view of No 4260 near final completion at Derby shows a wealth of detail which would be less easily visible in everyday circumstances. Information on detailing the Airfix '4F' is contained on page 22. *Ian Allan Library*

Right:

It should not be forgotten that along with the more prestigious new classes of locomotive introduced after the Grouping, for many years the LMSR operated a rich diversity of locomotives originally from the constituent companies. This view of former Highland Railway 'Skye Bogie' 4-4-0 No 14279 running light at Inverness in 1927 includes much of interest to the pre-Nationalisation modeller. Note in particular the variety of wagons in different company liveries. *H. C. Casserley*

MODELLING THE LMSR

Introduction

My first experience in, and, indeed, introduction to, the exciting world of model railways was by way of the LMSR. I lived firmly in Southern Railway territory, but the much desired Hornby 0 gauge tinplate train set which arrived at Christmas had as its motive power the familiar Hornby 0-4-0 tank engine in crimson lake, lined out and lettered in full LMSR style. It was soon joined by the 0-4-0 tender engine from the Hornby range, also the same finish. Its open top tender was the subject of my first ever model railway 'conversion'. I decided the model looked like no LMSR tender locomotive I could find in the Ian Allan *ABC books*, so I fitted a cardboard insert to make it resemble the tender of what was then the latest (and last) LMSR steam engine, the Ivatt Class 4 2-6-0 Mogul. That, of course, was in childhood, and in those days I had only a fleeting acquaintance with the LMSR on occasional trips north of London. I was more familiar with Southern and Great Western lines, and the lasting impression from early memories of the LMSR in its last few months of operation is of very black, very dirty, locomotives, and dirty passenger coaches with an ingrained smell of smoke in the upholstery. It was quite a contrast to the much cleaner Southern Electric.

The other impression, though, was of bustle and activity. Euston was an exciting place to be, with a great variety of locomotives large and small and a never ending movement of trains. Up the line there were huge yards and seemingly endless freight trains. So I was hooked on the LMSR and its functional 'no nonsense' locomotive and coach designs, and its association with the major cities of Great Britain. The LMSR had an air of urgency about its activities – getting on with a commercial job without worrying too much about its 'image', though its image was a good one, nonetheless, particularly in the late 1930s. No doubt the fact that it painted most of its locomotives black well before the other 'Big Four' companies did had something to do with the impression of a business-like company. Be that as it may, the London, Midland & Scottish Railway has always had a good following among model railway enthusiasts. The model trade has always supported the LMSR following as well, with plenty of ready-to-run items, kits, and accessories. In fact even a beginner can get going with a layout having a LMSR theme for there is plenty in the model shops to get you started.

In compiling this book the most obvious finding was just how vast a system it was because of the many constituent companies. So within these pages I have had to be selective and I have tried to give emphasis to aspects of the company that are of particular interest to modellers. There are many reference books on specific aspects of the LMSR and its pre-group constituents which are available for further study, and some of these are listed in the appendix. The photographs selected for this book are included for their value to modellers, and if some of the more obvious illustrations with a LMSR theme are omitted it is because they can be seen in other publications.

For assistance with the compilation of photographs and material for this book I would like to thank S. W. Stevens-Stratten, Malcolm Carlsson, Ray Hammond, Arthur North, Mike Trice, Richard Gardner, and Brian Monaghan. Thanks also to Jane Cartwright for assistance with typing the manuscript.

Chris Ellis

1 LMSR: A question of identity

Until 1 January 1923 the railways of Great Britain were a diverse conglomeration of companies, some big, some small, some well endowed and some completely run down. They were themselves mostly the product of the railway mania of the mid-19th century, when lines covering all parts of the land formed a network of great complexity, often duplicating or competing on major routes. The traveller, with the aid of a friendly booking clerk or the compendious *Bradshaw's Guide* could go almost anywhere in the land by train, for branch lines served rural areas well. Nonetheless, where rival companies did not co-operate there were minor inconveniences like having to cross town to transfer to another company's station. But in general there was a good service for the traveller.

Labour was cheap too, and the early years of the present century were the heyday of freight movement by rail. Again, there were goods yards everywhere, many owned by rival companies, although some were jointly owned.

Not all was well, however, and by the time the First World War started many companies were having a bad time financially. When the war started in 1914 the need to harness transport to the war effort led to the railway companies coming under government direction, though they retained their separate identities and managements.

But the writing was on the wall. Railway organisation in Britain was too complex and wasteful of resources. The war had caused great financial strain and some rail companies were in a poor state. The Railway Transport Act of August 1921 therefore directed that the many small companies should be grouped into new public companies, each broadly covering an area of the country, and absorbing the smaller companies in its area. Five areas were proposed, Scotland, West, Midlands, East and South. In the event, Scotland was dropped as a group company and its lines were taken over by the Midland and Eastern interests.

Thus on 1 January 1923, the Great Western Railway, the Southern Railway, London & North Eastern Railway, and finally the London, Midland and Scottish Railway – LMS, LM&SR, or LMSR for short came into being.

Of the grouping companies only the Great Western Railway kept its pre-1923 identity intact. This was because it already was the dominant company in the west. It was not so straight-forward, for the LMSR company, largest of the groupings, which was formed anew from a diverse number of companies. These ranged from some of the largest in Great Britain – the London and North Western, the Midland and the Caledonian – to some of the smallest, such as the Furness Railway and the North London Railway.

Below left:
The Midland Railway, later the Midland Division of the LMSR, was noted for its elegant small locomotives, as typified by 4-4-0 Class 2P with a fast train of only four ex-MR coaches in the early 1930s. Short train prototypes like this make the Midland Division a good choice for smaller layouts. *Ian Allan Library*

Bottom left:
However, the LMS Midland Division could also operate very long trains, as typified by 0-6-4T 'Flat Iron' No 2029 at Elstree with an eight-coach suburban train about 1926. The locomotive has the LMSR crest on the bunker side, the large Midland style numbers on the tank sides, and has the original MR initials from Midland days painted out on the buffer beam, with paint patches just visible. *Ian Allan Library*

Below:
The LMS image of the late 1930s; the magnificent and dramatic 'Coronation Scot' Euston-Glasgow express introduced in 1937 with the first of the 'Princess Coronation' class streamliners in charge. No 6220 *Coronation*. In blue with silver 'speed stripes', this train epitomised the LMSR at its peak. *Ian Allan Library*

Of all the groupings, the LMSR was the most difficult to organise into a corporate whole, for the major constituent companies involved had been deadly rivals prior to 1923. The London and North Western Railway styled itself the 'Premier Line' and had its headquarters at Crewe. It was also the largest of all the pre-grouping companies in financial terms. Its main London terminus was Euston and its main lines ran through Birmingham and Crewe to the northwest. There were routes into North and South Wales and the steam packet routes from Holyhead and Heysham to Ireland. It controlled the North London Railway and in 1922 it absorbed another big and well organised company, the Lancashire & Yorkshire, with whose routes the LNWR was, in any case, linked.

The rival Midland Railway was noted for its elegant small locomotives and its attractive crimson lake colour scheme. Its headquarters were at Derby and its London terminus was St Pancras. Its main route north was via Leicester and Nottingham, and it ran from there northwest to Manchester and east to Lincoln. It also ran west to Bristol and Gloucester, and to capture traffic to Scotland in rivalry to the LNWR it had built the famous Settle and Carlisle line, opened in 1876.

In 1912 it took over a famous local surburban company, the London, Tilbury & Southend Railway, and it jointly owned, with the London & South Western Railway, the Somerset and Dorset Railway which linked the Severn estuary to Bournemouth on the South Coast. Finally, in England it operated jointly with the Great Northern Railway, the Midland & Great Northern joint line. In Ireland the Midland had control of the 5ft 3in gauge Northern Counties Committee and County Donegal Joint Committee lines.

In Scotland, the LMSR absorbed the big Caledonian Railway, the Glasgow and South Western, and the Highland Railway. The first two of these companies were big and busy, both serving the Glasgow area and Lowlands. Another important constituent was the North Staffordshire Railway, while the LMSR also had a one third interest in the Cheshire Lines Committee, inherited from the Midland Railway's involvement before 1923. The new LMSR company found itself in 1923 as an immense and sprawling organisation whose routes ran from London and also extended eastwards. They reached into the southwest and extended up the west coast of Britain, crossed Scotland and went to the far north via Inverness. It inherited a huge mixture of locomotive types, a vast variety of rolling stock, and conflicting operating practices.

LMSR trains ran through every conceivable type of British terrain, from grimy industrial developments to moor and mountain. The LMSR was the little saddle tank locomotive shunting the wharves in Liverpool, and it was the majestic express train linking London and Glasgow in record time. It was the train taking office workers through the London rush hour, it was the long coal train trundling south from the coalfields, and it was the one-coach local train on a sleepy Scottish branch line.

As far as the modeller is concerned, the LMSR in miniature will suit every type of layout concept and the problem is not so much in the supply of models but in the realistic selection and application of them to suit a layout idea.

Top:
Closer to reality was the less-than-sparkling local train. This is a branch train at Oxenhope in October 1946, with an ex-MR 0-4-4T. The coaches are in 'austerity' finish – plain maroon with no lining out. *H. C. Casserley*

Centre:
One of the problems the LMSR faced in the early days is well shown here – the lack of big locomotives for the long haul from London to Scotland. Faced with competition from LNER with new Pacific types, the LMS in the late 1920s tried extending the range of the 4-4-0 Midland Compounds by fitting some with bigger tenders having a much extended coal capacity. The coaches near the locomotive are ex-LNWR, in LMSR colours, and the rest appear to be ex-Midland types. *Real Photographs*

Left:
The Midland Railway provided the dominant influence on LMSR colour schemes, motive power, stock, and nearly everything else in the early days of the grouping. The famous Derby Museum 0 gauge layout demonstrates a typical pre-grouping scene in the Derby area, but nothing in this view of the model – except the dress styles – would have changed very noticeably in the years immediately following the grouping. This layout shows the standard Midland fencing, water crane, and lamps in this view. *Brian Monaghan*

Think of a layout size – the space you have available – or if size is no limitation, your own ideal layout setting, and you can then find a part of the real LMSR operation that can be reproduced in miniature.

If you fancy the big sweeping scenic approach and have a railway room at your disposal, then the Settle and Carlisle or the West Highland routes come to mind as suitable inspiration. On the other hand, if you have only a tiny L-shaped corner site then an LMSR branch line such as Dursley, Glos, or one in North Wales would suit the most limited space.

If the London, Midland & Scottish Railway was easy to define as a company in business terms it was (and is) difficult to define in terms of equipment and style. For in truth there never was a completely 'standard' LMS. The company existed for exactly 25 years before it, in turn, became the London Midland Region of the nationalised British Railways on 1 January 1948. That 25 year period included a major recession (in roughly the 1929-1933 period) and a world war. During its existence big progress was made in the production of standardised LMSR locomotive and rolling stock designs, not to mention structures, signals and the like.

But much was inherited, and the constituent companies were so firmly entrenched in their ways that some parts of the LMSR changed hardly at all except in name and livery in 1923 when the grouping took place, and it is the whys and wherefores of this which we must consider next.

Top:

In British Railways days, this is Johnson Class 3F 0-6-0 No 43216 with its weather sheet in front protecting the crew as it runs tender-first with a single brake/3rd suburban standard coach. It is at Bawdrip Halt on the Bridgwater North-Edington Junction line just after nationalisation. It is an ex-Somerset & Dorset LMS-built locomotive fitted with automatic token pick-up apparatus on the tender side. The lamp arrangement for a stopping train was peculiar to the S&D line. The simple halt with grass-grown platform would make a perfect model subject for a very small layout. *O. H. Prosser*

Above:

The grand prospect; Liverpool Lime Street station in 1927 with taxis, trams, bustle, and grimy facades. The scene is dominated by the typical big station hotel – the North Western – but the scene stealer is the Punch & Judy show taking place on a traffic island in the foreground! *Ian Allan Library*

Centre left:

LMS quaintness; Irlams o' th' Height station just after the grouping and still displaying Lancashire & Yorkshire poster boards. Wood platform and substantial canopies add to the charm. *Ian Allan Library*

Left:

Typical LMS; Watford Junction in 1946 with plenty of activity, LMS standard fencing and paintwork, and what appears to be primitive coal and water facilities in the locomotive siding. *H. C. Casserley*

2 The LMSR scene

The modeller of the LMSR scene does not have such a straightforward path ahead as, say, the GWR or BR modeller. The great inheritance of locomotives and stock from widely differing, but quite large, companies, meant that all through the LMSR era it was possible to find areas or lines where very little changed from pregrouping days for the whole duration of the company's existence. To take an extreme example: on the Killin branch in Scotland which had been worked by the old Caledonian Railway company, the branch locomotive was invariably an ex-CR McIntosh 0-4-4T (occasionally a small ex-CR 0-6-0 tender engine might be substituted), the coaches were ex-CR and so were most of the very few goods wagons which were used on the branch. Only the LMSR paint schemes on the locomotive and stock, and LMSR lettering on the station signs changed with the times, and the branch was more or less pure Caledonian Railway in style and looks, despite the change of ownership. Things hardly changed in BR days (except for BR lettering) and it was not until the final days of steam in the early 1960s that a BR standard 2-6-2T tank locomotive displaced the Caley 0-4-4T.

Other examples can be cited in plenty – the Moffat branch (ex-CR), the Holywell Town branch (ex-LNWR), the Dursley branch (ex-MR), and so on – where pre-grouping locomotives and stock were in evidence through most of the 25 years of the LMSR and beyond. The old pre-grouping influence was everywhere, and although the LMSR did introduce standard locomotives and rolling stock, the settings in which they ran were mostly of pure pre-grouping character, even if the old pre-grouping locomotives and rolling stock were eventually replaced. Examples were everywhere to be seen, but there is only space to mention a few. One of them was the old Midland Railway main line north from St Pancras, where the neat stations were distinctly Midland Railway, complete with the diagonal standard MR fencing, throughout the LMSR period of ownership. Indeed, some of these stations, such as Radlett, are still scarcely changed today some 35 years or so after the LMSR ceased to exist, and more than 60 years after the Midland Railway disappeared! Only the name of ownership and the liveries and styles of the passing trains have changed. In the interim there may have been modern replacements or additions – new lamps, new huts, new signals etc – in a later style, but in essence that part of the LMSR still had the 'Midland' flavour.

By contrast, the London, Tilbury & Southend section of the LMSR which ran from Fenchurch Street in London, had its own distinctive locomotives, stock, and buildings inherited from the LTSR in 1912. Only slowly, in the 1930s, did LMSR standard locomotives and stock appear on the scene. But the whole atmosphere and 'look' of the LT&SR section was very different to the old Midland and main line from St Pancras. Destination boards on the front of the locomotives were a LTSR tradition which survived to the end of steam in BR days.

To this day, Manchester Victoria station is packed with the character and atmosphere of the old LYR, whose terminus it was, and, of course, it was even more like a Lancashire & Yorkshire outpost in later days when ex-LYR locomotives in LMSR colours would be the dominant types on view. Birmingham New Street, by contrast, was a pure LNWR station in style and looks until it was demolished in the 1960s to be replaced by the present modern station of that name. There are many more examples of places and stations where the pre-grouping 'look' lasted through the LMSR era and beyond. Leicester Central (MR), Euston (LNWR), Mallaig (CR) and Foxfield (FR) are random samples from dozens more.

When it came to locomotives and rolling stock, there was yet more pre-grouping influence to be seen system-wide. In some areas pre-group locomotives dominated the motive power scene for much of the lifetime of the LMSR (and beyond into nationalisation). As we shall see, the LMSR embarked on a big programme of standard designs for locomotives and rolling stock of all kinds and these were overlaid on the huge number of remaining pre-group types. The new standard designs turned up all over the system, but they were concentrated, initially at least, in the busiest and most important places, so there were areas where pre-group types were to be seen in large numbers throughout the LMSR period.

This was particularly the case in Scotland where the Caledonian's huge locomotive fleet remained particularly durable and long lived. Even into the 1950s it was possible to go train spotting on secondary lines in, say, the Lanark

Left:
For the modeller this casual snapshot taken at either Blackpool Central or South station c1931-32 is packed with fascinating detail which reveals the 'look' of a big LMSR station. The train indicator board is of a type which was common at LMS stations and was still seen in BR days. But note that it is from the pre-grouping era. Still marked 'LYR and LNWR Joint Railways'. Round the centre pillar is a clutter of slot and weight machines, and above them is a brand new Tannoy speaker installation (they were grey with black letters). There are metal advert panels randomly placed, even in the darkest and most obscure corners. The word 'Parcels' is obliterated by a paper strip above the left luggage office, and there is a neatly chalked train alteration board near the ticket barrier. The elegant buffet trolley dispenses tea in real cups and has a glass food case and pram-like wheels – it would make an attractive model. The LMSR advertising panels are black with white lettering, and the Tiny Signs company makes miniature versions of these. *Ian Allan Library*

Above:
A far west outpost of LMSR influence. Seen from the buffer stops this is the pretty little seaside station of Burnham-on-Sea, furthest point west for the Somerset & Dorset Railway, and having a brick built train shelter about one coach long, short platforms, and a simple track layout – a far cry from the usual LMS image. Platform at right without a shelter was used for seaside excursion trains – the regular branch trains used the left hand platform. *Colin Maggs*

area, and in the course of a day see *only* ex-Caledonian Railway locomotives. In LMSR days, too, locomotives running over ex-CR lines still carried the distinctive Caledonian route indicator semaphore on the front end.

So the modeller of the LMSR has to give much more thought to the setting of a layout than say, the GWR or the BR modeller. It is possible to build a fictional GWR layout to suit any part of that system, using standard GWR fittings and models. Possibly only the structures would reflect the area, but even these could be brick or wood to give a completely neutral setting which would, nonetheless, allow a thoroughly convincing GWR layout to be built. A modern BR layout could depict anywhere on the system if you were careful enough to reproduce new standard architecture in your station and sheds – it could be Milton Keynes or even Bristol Parkway, or any fictional place with this type of structure.

On the LMSR, however, there were relatively few new stations built during the company's tenure of office (though there *were* standard structures) and most areas reflected the styles and structures of the pre-grouping constituents. Thus you need to work out just where your layout is supposed to be. On former Midland territory? LNWR? Caledonian? Furness? All were markedly different in station and structure styles, and in detail fittings, yet all were LMSR in the 1923-48 period. There were big variations in scenic settings too, from the cosy wooded outer suburbs of Hertfordshire to the bleak windswept moors of the Settle and Carlisle line. There were the Lancashire and Yorkshire hills and a background of textile mills, coalmines, and cobbled streets. There were big industrial areas like Manchester and Liverpool, and associated sea ports. And there were the remote and picturesque main lines and branches in the Highlands of Scotland.

In fact, it is the vast range of possibilities that makes the LMSR an exciting company to model.

Top:
LMS suburban. The street entrance for Kilburn station is only just apparent among the row of high street shops which almost engulf it. The generally seedy air was not at all uncommon at minor suburban stations on the LMS system. *Ian Allan Library*

Centre:
To show that the LMSR was very much a railway of contrasts here is Blackwell station in Derbyshire, a former Midland structure. It is really a halt with local stone used for the platform facings and the shelter and walls. The name is on a wooden board by the shelter entrance. Note the branch line coming in from the right, with a '3F' and goods train descending a steep grade. *Locomotive Publishing Co.*

Above:
One of the most romantic of LMSR termini – Kyle of Lochalsh, a setting which has inspired many layouts in the past. The Class 5 heads the mid-morning train to Inverness, and the jetty is kept busy with cargo and passengers for the Western Isles. *C. P. Boocock*

Right:
The characteristic LMSR scene. Liverpool Edge Hill in the 1930s with a Midland Compound 4-4-0 No 1159 leaving with a short semi-fast train to Chester comprising of three of the standard LMS panelled coaches and an old LNWR coach. In the foreground a Class 3F 0-6-0T 'Jinty' is shunting the local freight yard and in the distance is a main sorting yard. Signals are LNWR standard types. *Real Photographs*

Above:
LMSR relics lingered well into the BR age. The nameboard and porter's trolley were still to be seen at Clapham, Beds, in 1968, although the black LMS style notice boards have disappeared.
J. Scrace

Below:
Virtually everything in this scene could be duplicated in miniature in 4mm scale. LMSR standard vans are in the Cadbury loading bay most of the private owner wagons are produced in miniature. The ED wagons are engineering department and Ratio produce kits of a similar type. Note that the Ricketts wagon on far left has white tyres. The scene is Finchley Road in the early 1930s. *Ian Allan Library*

At its peak of achievement in the late 1930s, the LMSR was a model of commercial and industrial progress. The locomotives then being built were second to none in balance and style, and reflected the 'state of the art' as far as British steam engineering was concerned. They were not necessarily the most ornately finished of machines, nor were they the most impeccably detailed, but they represented the best combination of functionalism and technical excellence in the tight economic conditions of the time. Even today, the fine locomotive designs of the 1930s – the 'Black Fives', the 'Jubilees', the 'Duchesses' and the 'Princess Coronations' do not look archaic as machinery. To modern eyes they look as functional and handsome as they did when they first appeared. Looking back through contemporary journals and popular railway books of the late 1930s it is no surprise to find the 'Princess Coronation' locomotives and the 'Coronation Scot' train the most widely illustrated of all British railway equipment. It was the image presented to the layman of British railway progress – just as the HST is today.

To see how the LMSR got that way we can start by looking at the motive power and its development, for this is well catered for in model terms.

Top right:

Another scene at Finchley Road in the 1930s. No 3559 is a Deeley rebuild of a Johnson 0-6-0 of 1885 vintage, typical of the assorted small locomotives of this type. The grimy state of the locomotive with its duty number on the lamp iron is also very characteristic. *Ian Allan Library*

Right:

The most typical LMS locomotive of them all was the Fowler '4F' 0-6-0, black, dirty, and hauling a long coal train. This view shows the smokebox number plate (the shed plate is almost obliterated by dirt) affixed to all locomotives and marked in white. *T. Lewis*

Below:

Shunting at Edge Hill in the early 1930s. The Jinty is still in the 1923 style freight locomotive finish with large tank numbers. The signals are LNWR standard types and of interest is the two-way signal for shunting purposes on the right. *Real Photographs*

Left:
More pre-grouping atmosphere. This is pure LNWR at Kings Langley with only the LMS crimson lake livery instead of LNWR livery to indicate the passage of time. No 25683 *Falaba* of the 'Prince of Wales' class, designed by Bowen Cooke and dating from 1915. It is of interest to note that Derby's Midland influence had not penetrated to the extent of fitting either a number plate or a shed plate on the smokebox of a Crewe engine. *C. R. L. Coles*

Centre left:
Late survival of the LMS look is shown here in February 1950, two years after nationalisation when 'Patriot' No 45516, *The Bedfordshire & Hertfordshire Regiment* leaves Southampton Docks with a troop train for Bedford carrying the men of the regiment after whom the locomotive was named. The locomotive has a BR number but is otherwise still in prewar crimson lake finish and well polished for the occasion. The train is composed of Gresley coaches still in LNER teak finish and Southern style route discs are carried, with the SR 'SPL' (Special) marking on one of them. The LMS style telegraphing number for a special is carried in the regulation place on the smokebox door. *S. C. Townroe*

Below:
LMSR style can be effectively shown on a layout. Richard Gardner's Linfield Junction is set in early BR days but in former LMS(LNWR) territory, complete with LNWR signals, LNWR standard station building (scratch-built), and LMS station nameboards. The later LMS standard signal box – brick with wood upper storey – can be seen and the ground frame hut is still in the old brown/stone colours.
Richard Gardner

Left:
The LMSR atmosphere can be recreated quite effectively from ready-to-run models available today. Hornby's Stanier 'Black Five' needs extra detailing to achieve perfection, and it is a scale foot too short, but it still manages to look the part in the mixed traffic livery of black lined in red. Hornby's Stanier 57ft standard coaches are seen in the background. *Hornby Hobbies*

Below left:
On the turntable of the layout of the Marlow & Maidenhead MRS is a nicely made Fowler '3F' converted from the Airfix 4F. The plain black dirty livery captures the LMS atmosphere immediately and is a positive help to the unskilled painter of models. *Chris Ellis*

Below:
These LNWR engineering department wagons are typical of many kits that are available for wagons in the LMS period. Models are 4mm scale from Ratio. *Chris Ellis*

Above:
Many kits of LMS locomotives supplement the ready-to-run models. This is McGowan's Stanier 6P No 6170 *Britsh Legion*, a rebuild of the old *Fury*, and actually a 'one off' though it was classed with the rebuilt 'Royal Scot' class. The kit is a set of body line castings to fit the old Airfix 'Royal Scot' chassis, all in 4mm scale.

Right:
LMS modernisation. A ferro-concrete loco coaling plant with wagon hoist and tippler as installed at several major MPDs in the 1930s – a fine subject for a straightforward scratch-building project. The loco coaling road ran between the legs of the tower.
Ian Allan Library

3 Motive Power

As we have seen, the LMSR in 1923 inherited a huge collection of miscellaneous locomotive types, 10,134 machines in total, ranging from large classes of standardised designs to ancient museum pieces or 'one-offs'. Unlike the other companies in the 'big four' grouping, the LMSR wavered in the development of new types for some years after 1923. This was largely due to the changes at the top level of management which veered in the direction of pre-grouping loyalties.

At the time of the grouping, the old power centres remained. The Midland division (essentially the old Midland Railway area) had its headquarters at Derby, and the North Western Division (the old LNWR/LYR combination) was centred on Crewe and Horwich. George Hughes, Chief Mechanical Engineer of the Lancashire and Yorkshire Railway, became the all-important Chief Mechanical Engineer of the new LMSR.

Hughes was innovative and forward looking. He believed in big and efficient locomotives and had already been responsible from some excellent L&YR designs. Hughes quickly designed a 2-6-0 as the first standard LMS, type basing his ideas for this on modern American locomotives of this type. He went on to draw up designs for a 2-10-0, a 2-8-2 and a 4-6-2 all intended as powerful standard types for the new company. Of these, only the 2-6-0 appeared. It was soon nicknamed 'Crab' on account of the prominent cylinders and valve gear which gave it a 'high stepping' gait. The 'Crab' was popular and useful and survived during the LMS period up to the later days of BR steam. A good cheap model in 00 gauge (which needs much reworking for greater accuracy) is produced by Lima, while Wills make a 4mm scale cast metal kit to fit a Hornby chassis.

Hughes retired in 1925 and was succeeded by Henry Fowler, his deputy, who had been CME of the old Midland company. The Midland Railway had favoured small engines of conservative style, and most of the management behind Fowler (including his locomotive superintendent) had come from the Midland Railway. Midland design philosophy then held sway and its stamp was impressed firmly on all new production. The Hughes 'Crabs', still under construction, were given the Midland standard tender (a poor match to the engine) as the very first move. But instead of more Moguls, Fowler turned the clock back and his old '4F' Midland Railway 0-6-0 goods engine was put back into production as a standard type, with over 770 being built in batches up to 1940, and including 192 MR locomotives built before 1923. The 'Plain Jane' '4F' was competent and conventional, utilitarian in its appearance and reliable enough except for occasional axle box trouble. It gave great service right up to the end of BR steam, and it could be seen everywhere on the system. It was, in fact, the archetypal British six-wheeler, and the one virtually every rail enthusiast can recognise.

The LMSR modeller with a small layout could get by with only one or two '4Fs' for they could do virtually every duty in real life – passenger haulage, yard shunting, pick-up goods, branch passenger, coal train and so on. Fortunately, for the 4mm scale modeller there is a truly excellent replica of the '4F' produced by Airfix/Mainline and arguably one of the best ready-to-run models ever produced in terms of accuracy and appearance. Models of the '4F' have also been produced by Lima in N and 0 scales though these are now out of production. Several '4F' kits exist however, and for any LMSR modeller, certainly in 4mm scale, a Fowler '4F' can go right to the top of the shopping list.

Fowler also perpetuated the handsome Midland Compound 4-4-0 as a standard design (190 built 1926-32 in batches), his 0-6-0T 'Jinty' shunter (530 built), and introduced a class 2P 4-4-0, virtually a simple version of the Compound. An old Midland type much in evidence, also, was the '3F' 0-6-0 tender engine, virtually a smaller version of the '4F'. Fortunately for the 4mm scale modeller there are (or have been) ready-to-run models of the

Above left:
The Midland influence prevailed under Fowler. The Midland Compound was one of a number of types subsequently repeated as a standard type in early LMS days. The LMS engines had left hand drive, but this former MR locomotive has the old Midland right hand drive. The 1928 style passenger livery of crimson lake, lined in black and straw yellow, is shown here to perfection, including the full lining to the wheels.
Ian Allan Library

Left:
Another Midland type which became ubiquitous over the LMS system was the Fowler Class 4F as over 700 were built up to 1940. This is a locomotive with left hand drive (note reversing lever and steam injector pipe) built by the LMS. It is in the plainest version of freight livery, black with straw yellow unblocked lettering. Note power class (4) marked high on the cab side.
Locomotive Publishing Co

Left:
The distinctive and very modern 2-6-0 'Crab' as designed by Hughes, the first LMS CME. It has a Midland tender which does not match the locomotive width. It has the lined out 1928 style mixed traffic livery with gold lettering fully blocked. *Locomotive Publishing Co*

Centre left:
The LMS managed with many old locomotives, despite the building of new standard classes by Fowler and Stanier. Here is a typical old-timer – a Johnson Class 2F rebuild of 1875 with a pick-up goods at Harper Lane bridge near Radlett in 1948. Noteworthy is the typical LMS practice of cleaning around the lettering and numbers, though as this locomotive had recently been renumbered the cab side area had probably been repainted, together, apparently, with the smokebox and chimney a typical example of LMS economy. *E. D. Bruton*

Bottom left:
One of the smallest of prototypes in model form is Dapol's ex-LYR 'Pug', a popular little shunter no longer than a wagon. Note that on the model as supplied the serifs on the numbers are too big and need touching out a little with black paint. *Chris Ellis*

Compound, Jinty '3F', and '3F', all from Hornby; a class 2P from Mainline; plus cast metal or etched brass kits for all of them. It must be said that other gauges are less well catered for, though Graham Farish produce a good N gauge Compound, and there are several 0 gauge kits of these types.

There was, in fact, a good case for standardising on Midland designs, for an analysis carried out early on found that the locomotives were simpler to build, and could be maintained at a lowest cost; and they were economical to run. Also, there were already around 3,000 locomotives of '4F', '3F' and '2P' type inherited from the Midland Railway. The LMS-built versions differed mainly in being arranged for left-hand drive as adopted for the LMS rather than the right-hand drive of the MR locomotives.

Hughes, and his successor Fowler, did in fact have plans for larger locomotives, including 4-6-0, 4-6-2 and 2-8-2 compounds, but the Midland-influenced operating department were not enthusiastic. However, during this period of indecision, the rivals to the LMS had all produced headline-stealing express locomotives – the GWR 'Castle' 4-6-0, SR 'King Arthurs' and 'Lord Nelsons' and the LNER Gresley Pacifics. A GWR 'Castle' was borrowed in 1926 by the LMSR and showed a dramatic improvement over the best performances of the existing LMSR express types. In order not to fall behind for 1927, the management ordered a 'crash' programme of 50 4-6-0s to be built 'off the drawing board' by the North British Locomotive Co – and the SR Lord Nelson class drawings were among those borrowed to help speed up the design.

Despite being conceived and built in great haste, the 'Royal Scot' class 4-6-0s proved extremely successful, and they not only provided the LMSR at last, with a big modern express locomotive type – eliminating double-heading by two 4-4-0s for example – but they captured the public eye and created a favourable 'image' for the LMSR just as the

rival companies had enjoyed with their big engines. Mainline produced an excellent 4mm scale model of an original 'Royal Scot' which exactly reproduced the majesty of the design. A Rivarossi model was also made a few years ago, but unfortunately it was to a 'bastard' scale of 3.8mm to 1ft, making it virtually unsuitable for use with either H0 or 00 scale models.

Some 70 'Royal Scot' class locomotives were built in two batches. Smoke deflectors were soon added and detail changes were made. In the 1930s many were given later type tenders and later still rebuilding changed the appearance even more. The modeller's main concern, given that an excellent 4mm scale ready-to-run replica is available, is to get the details, colour scheme, name and number, correct for the period being modelled. Closely following the 'Royal Scot' Fowler produced the 'Patriots' which were nominally rebuilds of old LNWR 'Claughton' 4-6-0s. They were popularly known as 'Baby Scots'. Hornby make a 4mm scale model.

Another notable design of the Fowler regime was the huge 2-6-0+0-6-2 Beyer-Garratt articulated freight locomotives specifically intended for the heavy coal trains that ran south on the Midland Division lines from Toton to Brent. Again, the need was for big power to eliminate double-heading. Hughes had initiated this idea – the firm of Beyer-Peacock were the builders – but Fowler was in charge when they were ordered, and in consequence some standard outmoded details were incorporated – short travel valve gear and inadequate axle bearings – which limited the potential of these big machines. They could have been even more spectacular than they looked, and more economical. Naturally, Beyer-Garratts have always excited modellers and there have over the past 20 years or so

Top left:
The famous 'Royal Scot' class is thought of as an express passenger type, but it could be found on freight work during fill-in turns. Here in BR days No 46122 *Royal Ulster Rifleman* passing Oxford on a freight from Cowley to Merseyside in May 1962 in lined green livery. *Ian Allan Library*

Centre left:
Another example of a 'Royal Scot' on a minor train. In original condition is No 6165 *Ranger* in pristine condition and with the small Fowler tender. It is working a local train to Euston with a van next to the locomotive, and an assortment of pre-group coaches. The LNWR style shed plate is mounted on the smokebox door (below the number plate) and has black numbers on a white background; in this case '16' indicates Longsight. Ex-LNWR locomotives carried this style of shed plate on the cab rear (tank locos) or the rear rim of the cab roof. *Ian Allan Library*

Left:
LMSR resplendent. This is No 6100 *Royal Scot* as specially prepared for the 1933 tour of the USA and Canada. It was originally No 6152 but changed identities with the original No 6100 for the trip, and staying as No 6100 thereafter. The vast amount of polished steel, clearly evident here, would present a good modelling project, for a ready-to-run *Royal Scot* could be transformed in appearance if finished like this. *British Rail*

been 4mm scale kits from Kitmaster (plastic) and Ks (metal), while specialist suppliers have offered brass etched or limited production models.

The other design of great importance developed by Fowler, and one of his best, was the '2300' class 2-6-4T '4P' tank engine, some 125 of which were built in the 1927-34 period. The layout owed much to the Hughes 'Crab' 2-6-0 design and the resulting locomotive was just as effective and reliable. One of the very best Hornby 4mm scale ready-to-run models is of this type, produced in both LMSR red and black versions. For the N-gauge enthusiast there is an excellent Gem cast metal kit to fit a Graham Farish chassis. This type was mainly used on suburban passenger services, but it could also be seen on freight and parcels trains, and on station pilot duties.

A 2-6-2T reduced size version of the same design proved much less successful, being under-powered and only just adequate for the branch line passenger work (including push-pull) for which the class was intended. There is no ready-to-run model of this one, but there have been kits, including one in 4mm scale from Ks.

Among other Fowler types worth mentioning are the class 7F 0-8-0, which looked like a bigger '4F' but was actually a 'Midlandised' version of the LNWR 'G2' standard freight engine which the LMSR inherited in large numbers. There was a version of the 'Tilbury Tank' 4-4-2T built by the LMSR especially for the LT&S service, the famous 0-10-0 Lickey Banker 'Big Bertha', built by the MR in 1919, and the 2-8-0 built for the Somerset & Dorset Joint Railway both before and after the grouping. Kits and models of these types have been produced over the years, but not in ready-to-run form.

One last standard type LMSR locomotive which is produced in ready-to-run form is available only to N gauge modellers – the little

Centre right:

Another unusual finish was displayed by the name locomotive of the Jubilee class. To commemorate the Silver Jubilee of HM King George V in 1935, Stanier's new 3-cylinder 4-6-0s were thus named, and the first, No 5552 was given a special finish with polished steel top feed cover, much polished chrome trim, chrome boiler bands and raised metal letters and numbers, with a black livery. *Real Photographs*

Right:

Sentinel geared locomotives were taken into service for shunting duties, due to their economic operating costs. No 7164 was one of a batch of the smallest size. This one has an unusual colour scheme, lined out black apparently in the old LNWR style. *Ian Allan Library*

Above:

One of the most important of LMSR locomotives was Stanier's classic 'Black Five', a 2-cylinder 4-6-0 which was similar to the GWR 'Hall', but with outside valve gear and a less ornate finish. No 5044 was one of the early locomotives, built by Vulcan Foundry, and photographed to show all the details before going into service. It is in the black livery with red lining (though some were plain black). Note the 5P/5F power class on the cab side. *Ian Allan Library*

Left:

Two old ex-Midland types on shed at Kettering in the late 1930s. No 3042 is a rebuild of a Johnson '2F' of 1878 – the cab and Belpaire firebox are later changes – and 20216 is a Johnson '1P' 2-4-0 of 1876. A 4mm scale kit of this engine has been produced by Ratio. *C. R. L. Coles*

Below:

Stanier's first attempt at a 4-6-2 Pacific for the LMS – No 6200 *The Princess Royal*, name locomotive of the class when new in 1933. A high-side tender was later fitted, as was a dome forward of the top-feed. Hornby make a 4mm scale model of the locomotive in this condition. *Ian Allan Library*

Left:
The 'Princess Royals' were followed by the streamlined 'Princess Coronation' class which had their streamlined casing removed during and after World War 2. This is No 6248 *City of Leeds* de-streamlined and in the 1946 style passenger finish – black lined straw and crimson lake, and with 'Block' style lettering. The smokebox top was curved down to clear the streamlined shroud. *Real Photographs*

Left:
Prior to the 'Royal Scot' and Stanier's modern 4-6-0 and 4-6-2 types, the biggest locomotives for passenger service on the LMS were the old LNWR 4-6-0s. This is a 'Claughton', No 6013, in June 1931 working the top express of the day the 'Lancastrian'. It is taking water at speed from Castlethorpe troughs. *Leslie Thompson*

0-6-0T 'Dock' tank which is attractively modelled in the Hornby-Minitrix range.

Sir Henry Fowler retired in 1931 leaving a legacy of good looking but utterly conventional and conservative designs, many of which continued to give yeoman service almost to the end of steam traction in Great Britain. His successor was William Stanier (later Sir William) who came to the appointment of Chief Mechanical Engineer of the LMSR in January 1932, from being assistant to C. B. Collett, CME of the Great Western Railway. Under Stanier's guidance the motive power situation of the LMSR was transformed to provide the company with a range of locomotives which were collectively in design and engineering terms the best in the land. Coaching stock was also improved in commensurate style.

Stanier retained well established Fowler types, such as the '4F', which was produced in batches up to 1940. He continued the '4P' '2300' class 2-6-4T, but with his own improvements, and he began a new generation of high power locomotives to carry on from the 'Royal Scot' class. Stanier used the best of Great Western design practice – the tapered domeless boiler with top feed (though a dome was soon incorporated), and the neat proportions and fittings. He omitted the decorations like brass beading and capping, simplified the layouts to give outside cylinders

for ease of maintenance, and accepted simpler production practices, like mushroom-head rivets instead of flush rivets to keep costs down at a time of harsh economic restrictions.

The first Stanier design to reflect all this was the '5F' Mogul 2-6-0 of 1933, merely a version of the Hughes 'Crab' built to Stanier's design philosophy. Kits in 4mm scale have been produced of this type, but it was a locomotive of no great distinction.

The big impact in 1933 was made by the first two LMSR Pacifics, 6200 *The Princess Royal*, and 6201 *Princess Elizabeth* of the 'Princess Royal' class. These were the first locomotives to put the LMSR on level terms with the LNER Gresley Pacifics and the GWR 'Kings'. Indeed, Stanier based the boiler and chassis dimensions of *The Princess Royal* on his experience with the 'Kings', and there is some resemblance in the frontal aspects. Very fine 4mm scale models of these first two 'Princess Royals' are made in 4mm scale by Hornby (the old Tri-ang concern). An 0 gauge tinplate model was the most prestigious pre-war offering in the Hornby range (in Meccano days).

Stanier followed Fowler's 'Baby Scots' with a version of his own – a 3-cylinder 4-6-0 of similar dimensions but with the taper boiler and a new cab. Initially, these proved disappointing due to inadequacies in the boiler and draughting arrangements but, once these

problems were sorted out, the 'Jubilees' as they were called (to honour the Silver Jubilee of King George V), proved very efficient and more than 190 were built. There were variations in these, both with regard to boiler fittings and tenders. The old standard LMSR Fowler tender was initially fitted, followed by a new design of standard tender by Stanier with high curved sides. A few had an interim Stanier design with high flat sides. Mainline have produced several excellent 4mm scale versions of the 'Jubilee' class with the different tender combinations and varying colour schemes. Peco offer a very good N gauge version, and there have been cast metal kits from several manufacturers.

Stanier's greatest locomotives were to come, however. First of these was the celebrated 'Black Five' – the 4-6-0 mixed traffic engine, first built in 1934, rated 5P5F, and intended as a 'go anywhere' machine. It was essentially similar to the GWR 'Hall' class (which Stanier had helped design in his GWR days) but with outside valve gear and simpler construction. Some 842 were built over the years to 1951, a massive class of locomotives which were used all over the system and even beyond it. It was the definitive LMS engine apart from the '4F' 0-6-0, and could be seen on every sort of service from pick-up goods to express passenger train.

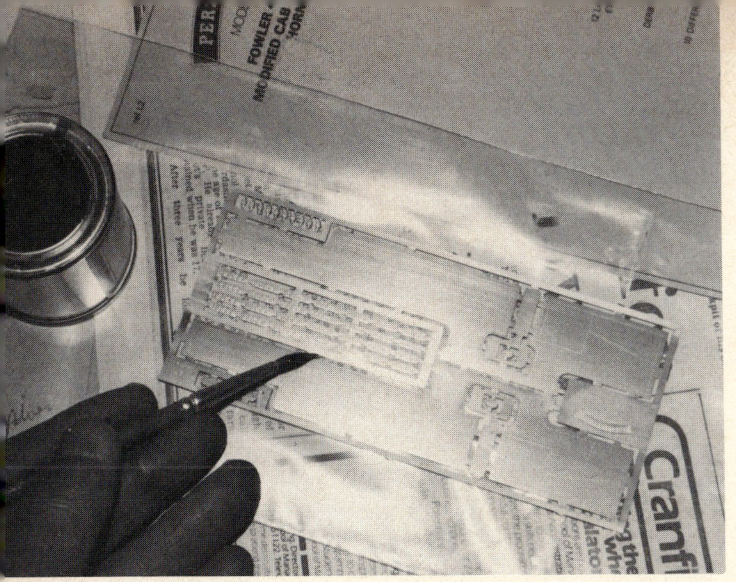

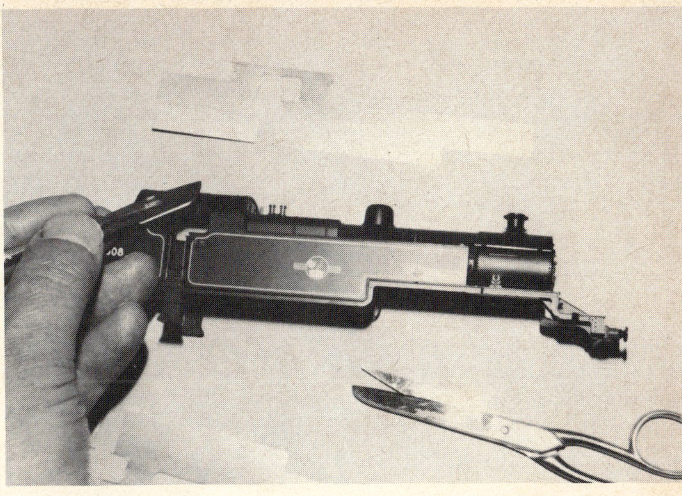

Above left:

The Perseverance fret containing the new sides and number and shed plates must be given a coat of etch primer before the pieces are cut from the fret.

Above:

The side pieces are then cut from the fret and the existing locomotive sides are trimmed and sanded flush, removing rain strips, etc.

Left:

Assembly work is then quite easy. Here the new sides are glued over the plastic sides, and a new chimney and outside steam pipes are added from the kit, as are new tank vent pipes. Washout plugs are drilled into the firebox side and small handrails are made from wire.

Below left:

Model is painted in plain freight black with straw yellow markings from Kingprint dry decal sheets. The chassis is dirtied and much grime and weather staining has been added. Crushed coal is glued in the bunker. The bogie brakes are covered over by adding a false side frame over each.

Below:

Another detail variation on the same theme. Using the same Perseverance kit another model is finished as No 2376 in the mixed traffic scheme of black lined red and with gold blocked lettering. This one retains the original chimney and short tank vents of the earlier machines and lacks the outside brake pipe steam pipes. Check individual locomotive details when carrying out conversion work, preferably only modelling a locomotive for which you can find reference photographs in books, etc.

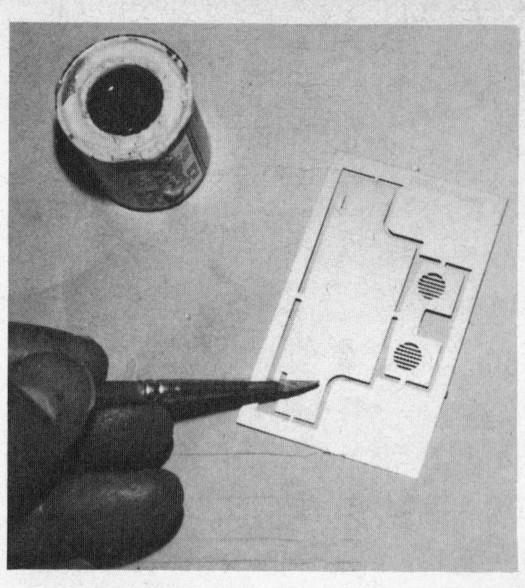

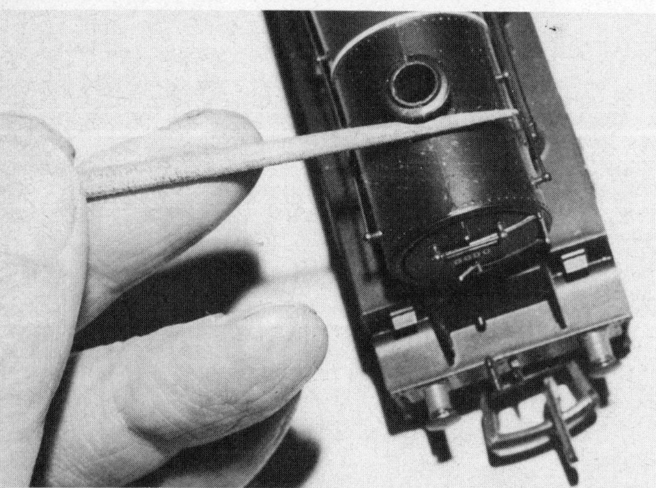

Top:
This is the Airfix/Mainline 4mm scale 0-6-0 Fowler 4F, looking good as purchased but capable of further variation and extra detailing.

Top right:
One immediate variation is the 4F with tender cab, and Perseverance produce an etched fret for a quick and precise assembly job.

Centre left:
Coal rails are added to the tender from Microstrip (though etched coal rails may be purchased), the piston tail rod covers are cut off for late period LMS, and join lines on the moulding are cleaned up. In this case a paper clip is used to replace the drawbar and so give a closer coupled tender.

Centre right:
Here is the finished model, complete with crew and a rather worn faded finish. Note how the wheels and motion have been dirtied up. (Compare with the first picture in this sequence to see the changes made.)

Above left:
Even the well-detailed Mainline models lend themselves to a little extra work to give them added character. On the 'Jubilee' *Leander* a file is used to remove traces of plastic mould lines.

Above:
Drill out lifting holes in the frames and add other minor details, plus larger balance weights from paper, seen here in white.

Left:
Add rest of cab detail including lip below cab roof.

Liverpool-Southport line was electrified by the Lancashire & Yorkshire Railway as early as 1904. The Midland followed by electrifying the Lancaster-Morecambe route in 1908 (using overhead catenary rather than a third rail). The LNWR electrified its suburban lines as far as Watford in 1913, originally with a fourth rail so that the Bakerloo line underground trains could share the route to Watford on the surface. The Manchester-Bury route was electrified by the LYR. Then in LMSR days the Manchester-Altrincham and the Wirral lines were electrified.

In the field of diesel traction the LMSR took a pioneering lead and started using small diesel locomotives for shunting in the 1930s. Their first effort was a 'home built' job using the frames and chassis of a '1F' 0-6-0T with a box-cab body, the finished locomotive looking something of a hybrid. A selection of industrial diesel types was purchased from Hunslet and others for experience and trials.

In 1935 some big 350hp diesel shunters were ordered from English Electric/Hawthorn Leslie, and in modified form this type was a direct predecessor of the BR Class 08 shunter still very familiar today.

In the immediate postwar period it was decided by the LMSR that passenger haulage could be dieselised and this led to the two LMS-built main line diesel locomotives Nos 10000 and 10001, the first of which was completed in 1947 just before nationalisation.

Other LMSR diesel types included three Leyland petrol railcars (in 1934), a three-coach fast suburban set built just prewar, and the Karrier road-railer, a motor coach adopted for rail running on special wheels. Models of LMS diesels and electrics are few and far between. Most readily available is the BR Class 08 diesel shunter which both Wrenn and Lima produce in 4mm scale. This is sold in LMS colours but needs detail changes to make the model accord with the correct details of the 7120 batch which dates from 1944. There are very few models available of other LMSR diesels and electrics, though Q Kits produced a resin bodied 10000 kit, and Ks produce the Karrier Road/railer as an attractive cast metal kit.

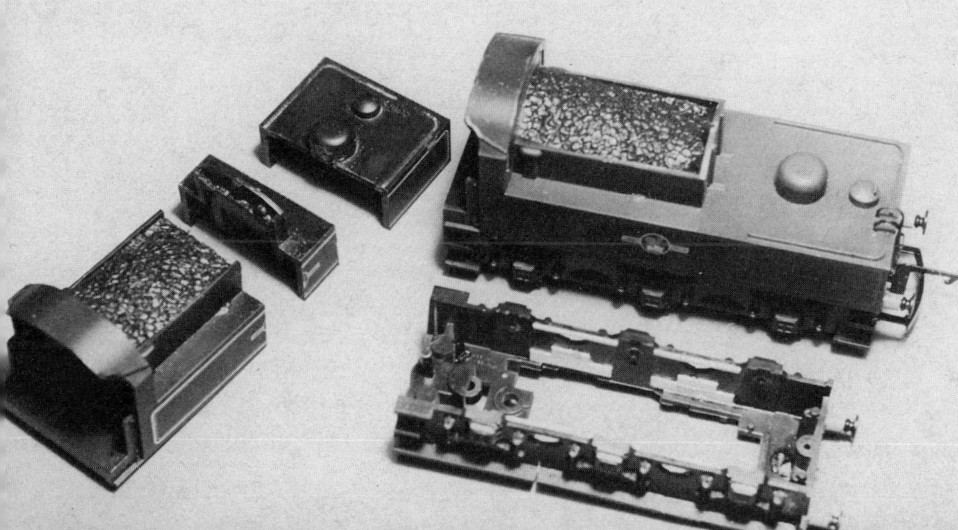

Dirty the chassis and motion, and add some grime if required. This tones down the crimson lake finish considerably and gives a realistic effect.

Above left:

The Hornby Ivatt Class 2 2-6-0 suffers from crude detail and an overscale tender which is stretched to fit a standard chassis. Gerald Scarborough transformed the model by adding extra detail, replacing the moulded handrails with wire, and cutting down the length of the tender. The 1946 'Block' style lettering is correct for this engine. *Gerald Scarborough*

Left:

Here is the Ivatt Class 2 tender dismantled, with a slice sawn out, and thus reduced to scale length. *Gerald Scarborough*

23

LMS 1245

Above:
Gerald Scarborough made the Ivatt Class 2 2-6-2T from the 2-6-0 Ivatt Class 2 tender locomotive by Hornby.

Right:
Plastic card is used to build side tanks, roof, and bunker. The cab rear comes from the tender cab.

Below right:
Underside view of the Ivatt 2-6-2T shows new rear frame. Spare Hornby leading truck is used for the trailing truck.   *Gerald Scarborough*

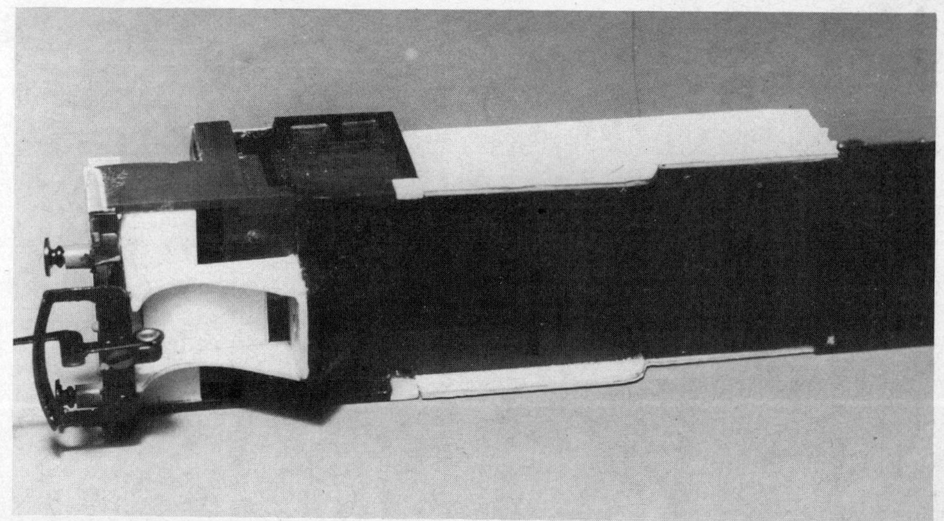

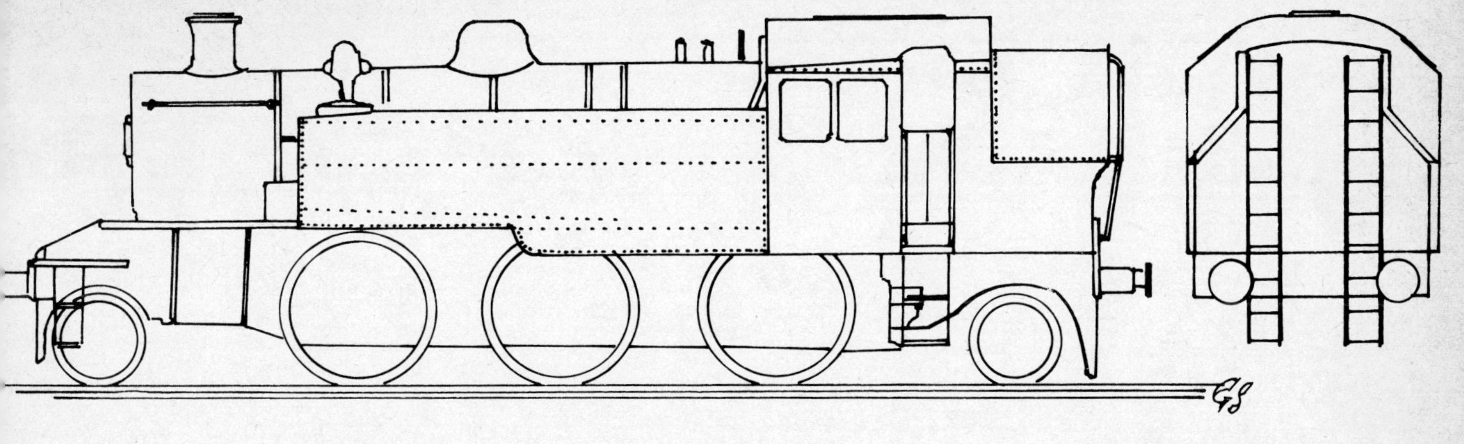

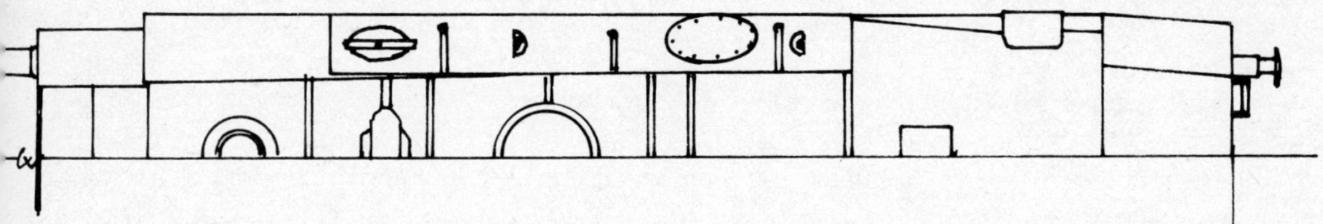

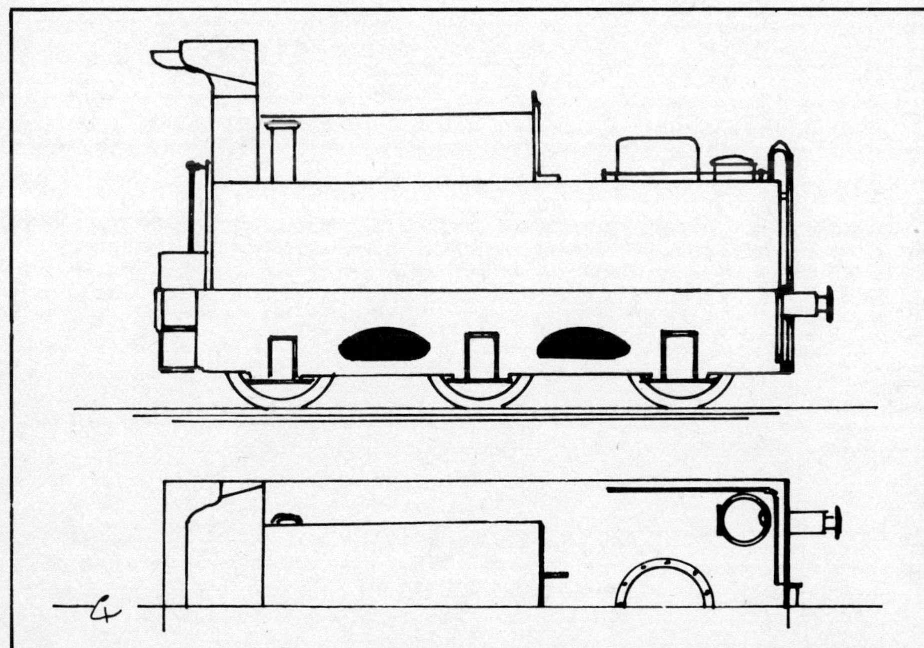

Above:
4mm scale working drawing for the Ivatt Class 2 2-6-2T conversion featured on page 24.
Gerald Scarborough

Left:
4mm scale drawing for Ivatt tender conversion featured on page 23. *Gerald Scarborough*

Below left:
Malcolm Carlsson converted the Roco English Electric export version of the diesel shunter to the LMS 7120 series version of 1944. Here is the basic model with new handrails, new side lockers, sandboxes, and lamp irons.

Below:
The end lights of the export version are removed and replaced by small lights and lamp irons.

Right:
The completed model in LMS black with straw yellow plain lettering. The 4mm scale Lima or Wrenn versions of the BR diesel shunter can be similarly detailed for the LMS version, matching the details to this model.   *Malcolm Carlsson*

Centre:
Hornby's 4mm scale model of *The Princess Royal* as in 1933 is a good likeness to this famous locomotive.

Bottom:
The Mainline model of a parallel boiler 'Royal Scot', No 6127 *The Old Contemptibles* is a good looking model even as purchased.

Left:
One of the more complex Crownline conversion kits is the set of metal parts for altering the Hornby 'Duchess' into one of the final engines of the class as modified by Ivatt. *Richard Gardner*

Below:

The parts from the Crownline conversion kit have here been added to the Hornby 'Duchess' which has been suitably altered to take the replacement parts. Note in particular the new trailing truck and ash-pan and under-cab changes. *Crownline*

Ready to run models – a selection

Class	Wheel type	Scale/ gauge	Maker	Period of livery	Remarks
4F	0-6-0	00	Airfix/Mainline	1928 on	Easy detail variations possible
0F	0-4-0ST	00	Dapol	1928 on	Ex-LYR 'Pug'
2300	2-6-4T	00	Hornby	1928 on	Produced in crimson and lined black versions
'Duchess'	4-6-2	00	Hornby	1938 on	
'Princess Royal'	4-6-2	00	Hornby	1934 on	Early tender
'Midland Compound'	4-4-0	00	Hornby	1928 on	Ex-MR type (No 1000)
'Patriot'	4-6-0	00	Hornby	1930 on	Tender is inaccurate and needs correcting
7120	0-6-0 diesel	00	Lima	1944 on	Needs correct detailing from BR body
5MT	4-6-0	00	Hornby	1934 on	
5MT	4-6-0	N	G. Farish	1934 on	
Rebuilt 'Scot'	4-6-0	00	Mainline	1946 on	Late livery
'Royal Scot'	4-6-0	00	Mainline	1930 on	Two types of tender
'Jubilee'	4-6-0	00	Mainline	1936 on	
Rebuilt 'Patriot'	4-6-0	00	Mainline	1936 on	Two versions with two tenders
2P	4-4-0	00	Mainline	1928 on	
8F	2-8-0	00	Wrenn (ex Hornby Dublo)	1934 on	
2MT	2-6-0	N	Hornby-Minitrix	–	(1) BR finish
2MT	2-6-2T	N	Hornby-Minitrix	–	(1) BR finish
OF	0-6-0T	N	Hornby-Minitrix	–	(1) BR finish
'Duchess'	4-6-2	N	G. Farish	1938 on	
'Compound'	4-4-0	N	G. Farish	1938 on	
'Jubilee'	4-6-0	N	Peco	1936 on	
4F	0-6-0	0	Lima	–	(2) BR finish

Notes

1. Only available in BR finish.
2. Limited availability.

Kits – a selection

Note that kits vary enormously in quality and degree of difficulty or simplicity. Listing here does not imply ease of construction. The selection is of important or interesting types not available in ready-to-run form. There are more kits available than are listed here, but note that fluctuating market conditions can also cause some kits to be withdrawn or be in short supply at times.

Class	Wheel type	Scale/gauge	Maker	Remarks
Sentinel	0-4-0	N	P & D Marsh	Fits Farish DMU motor bogie
Coal Tank	0-6-2T	4mm	Ks	Ex-LNWR standard type
Ro-Rail	Bus	4mm	Ks	Bus for road or rail running, Karrier 1930
2P	2-6-2T	4mm	Ks	Fowler branch line tank engine
2P	2-6-2T	4mm	Ks	Ivatt version of the above
2F	0-6-0	4mm	Ks	Johnson goods engine
5	4-6-0	4mm	Ks	Stanier 'Black Five' More accurate than Hornby r-t-r model
4	2-6-0	4mm	Ks	Stanier Mogul
Beyer-Garratt	2-6-0+0-6-2	4mm	Ks	Largest LMSR loco – articulated type
7P	4-6-2	4mm	Ks	Streamlined Pacific. More accurate than Hornby r-t-r version
0F	0-4-0ST	4mm	Ks	Johnson shunter
10000	Co-Co	4mm	Q Kits	Resin body
2P	2-4-0	4mm	Ratio	All plastic kit
3P	0-6-4T	4mm	Wills	Bodyline kit for Hornby chassis
4	2-6-0	4mm	Millholme	Ivatt Mogul
Dreadnought	4-6-0	4mm	Millholme	Ex-LYR design
7P	4-6-2	N	Langley	Fits Farish chassis
Turbomotive	4-6-2	N	Langley	Fits Farish chassis
7F	0-8-0	N	Gem	Fits Farish chassis
4F	0-6-0	N	Gem	Fits Farish chassis
4P	2-6-4T	N	Gem	Fits Farish chassis
Royal Scot	4-6-0	N	Langley	Fits Farish chassis
3F	0-6-0	N	Gem	Ex-LYR type
Sentinel	Railcar	N	Langley	Steam railcar
Pug	0-4-0ST	7mm	Sevenscal	Ex-LYR

4 Rolling Stock

The LMSR modeller does not, perhaps, do as well as the GWR enthusiast when it comes to rolling stock, though for the person with a layout of almost any size there will be no problem about stocking it adequately with highly authentic models of good quality from ready-to-run and plastic kit sources alone. Add to that the cast metal and etched brass kits available and you have a good selection. That is for 4mm scale – workers in other scales have rather more spade-work to do.

Take coaching stock first. For 4mm scale there is almost an embarrassment of riches.

Even if we disregard short run or specialist etched brass kits (and they are to be had, of course), there is first of all the Ratio range. It offers excellent kits of Midland Railway coaches, as well as those of the London & North Western Railway which were used through all of the LMS period and would be perfect for branch line trains. They are all prototypes of the early 1900s which could still be seen as late as 1950-52. They have the advantage of being models of short prototypes, always useful on small layouts. Also they have conversion potential to other

variations. Cast metal kits for some standard LNWR four-wheelers are made by Ks and these are valid, also, for early LMSR days.

For the LMS-built coaches there are some excellent 4mm ready-to-run examples. Before considering these, however, it is timely to stress that the fluctuations in the market during recent years means that quite a lot of models go out of production either temporarily or for good. A lot are made overseas for major ranges. Those mentioned here may not be on a retailers list at any given time, but most recent models can be found somewhere, even if they not appear in current catalogues. Three particular LMSR ranges are worth every effort to obtain. First of these are the old Airfix items (now absorbed into the Mainline range and also sold as Mainline models). The first are a pair of two Stanier 57ft non-corridor coaches of 1936 vintage, a brake/3rd and a 1st/3rd composite. These are flush-sided steel standard stock, as produced for secondary service – local and suburban trains, etc.

Complementing these, Airfix also produced the Stanier 60ft corridor 1st/3rd of the same period, and the 57ft Brake/3rd corridor as used on express and principal passenger services. Hornby also produced models of this type, but they do not have the same degree of detail and accuracy as the later Airfix designs. When Airfix disappeared as a separate company their models were mostly incorporated into the Mainline range, and the LMSR coaches were duly re-released in Mainline style. It is of further interest to note that Hornby also released their coaches of this type in the handsome 'Coronation Scot' livery of 1937, to match their 'Princess Coronation' class streamlined Pacific. These enable a representative train to be run, but modellers wanting the authentic nine coach set would need to do considerable converting and scratch-building to cover the other coaches in the set which Hornby do not offer (open 1st, open 3rd, dining car, kitchen car, etc).

Both Hornby and Airfix/Mainline also released these Stanier corridor coaches in the 'crimson lake and cream' livery of the early BR period, and the overall maroon of the late 1950s.

Mainline themselves, happily, did not duplicate the products of others. They produced two extremely fine models of the original standard LMS corridor coaches of wood-panelled type built in the period 1923-27. These are the brake/3rd and 1st/3rd composite, both very accurate. These were the types used on expresses until well into the 1930s – including the original 'Royal Scot' train. Thereafter they were used on less

Top:
4mm scale standard 57ft Stanier 1st/3rd non-corridor lavatory coach by Airfix/Mainline.

Centre:
4mm scale Stanier 60ft standard 1st/3rd from Airfix/Mainline range.

Left:
4mm scale Stanier full passenger brake from Mainline.

Rugby-Warwick push-pull train, in August 1950, composed of Stanier 57ft compartment stock hauled by an elderly (and visibly sagging) ex-LNWR 2-4-2T. The train still retains full LMS identity throughout. *H. Weston*

Though not 100% accurate in detail, the Hornby Royal Mail coach is an attractive working accessory which allows a famous LMS operation – the 'Night Mail' – to be reproduced in miniature.

A private owner coal wagon that ran on the LMS system. Note that this newly refitted Bolsover wagon has solebars in body colour, ironwork in black, and is marked with specific collieries to which it may be returned empty. The white tyres were sometimes seen on new wagons though they soon lost their brightness. For authenticity choose model PO wagons applicable to LMSR territory. *Ian Allan Library*

Top:

A typical ready-to-run 4mm scale private owner wagon. It looks good but rides on a non-authentic standard chassis.

Above:

The same wagon with improvements to greatly enhance its scale appearance. Aside from scale couplings (a matter of choice) it has ironwork picked out in black, is lightly weathered, and has the chassis altered to more accurately resemble the original wagon. This particular model is also converted for P4 running. Note the wheels are changed to disc type. *Mike Trice*

important routes but were still to be seen well into the 1960s on secondary trains. Detailed to perfection, these would be a safe purchase for any LMSR 4mm scale layout. BR 'crimson lake and cream' versions have also been produced.

Also counted as coaching stock are models of a Stanier period full passenger brake van and a parcels van from Mainline and Lima respectively. Apart from their availability in authentic LMSR liveries, they are produced also in early and late period BR finishes.

The LMSR freight stock scene in 4mm scale is not so well supplied with wholly authentic models as the passenger scene. There is no lack of LMSR models in the ready-to-run field, but in many cases these are a compromise, for the r-t-r models tend to use a common chassis for production economy, so that though the bodywork and markings may be wholly accurate the chassis is nondescript.

Most modellers in truth, conveniently overlook this discrepancy and happily accept the 'near-enough' chassis offered by the makers. However, the firm of Crownline supplies conversion parts for correct LMS brake gear, and some detail improvement is possible using plastic Microstrip or scrap plastic to make new brake gear.

The nature of the problem may be seen by studying a couple of examples. The Mainline 'Large' LMSR cattle wagon is a good example. In body detail, finish and number it is very authentic. But in order to fit the Mainline wagon chassis the body has been slightly compressed in length. The original had a wooden chassis with solebars and buffer beams painted body colour – but the model has a steel type chassis painted all black and the position and layout of the brake gear and rigging bears little resemblance to the original.

Compare also the photographs of the actual BISC ore wagon and a model from Mainline. This was a private owner wagon running on LMSR metals. The standard steel type chassis of the model is much closer to the real thing than most, but, again, the brake rigging is not like the real wagons, nor are the axleboxes. The end foot rungs are missing from the model chassis too. All of which should serve to indicate the depth of the problem, for discrepancies like these are repeated on nearly every model and some fruitful work can be done by the modeller, tracking down the errors and correcting them.

In the field of kits the modeller fares much better. Virtually all are correctly detailed in the chassis area.

Of the kit ranges available, three are particularly useful to the LMSR enthusiast. First Slaters produce a superb range of wagons in both 7mm and 4mm scale, plastic assembly kits which go together well and run superbly. Almost everything is duplicated in both scales and nearly every model is either a Midland or LMS type or a private owner wagon which ran on their metals. Very distinctive models in this range are the high-side Midland coke wagon, the standard 'large' cattle van, the Midland standard brake van (also used in LMSR days) and the standard 3-plank low-side MR/LMSR open wagon, but there are many more.

The ABS/Wrightlines firm does a range of metal cast kits also in both 7mm and 4mm scales. They include several LMSR types, notably the standard 5-plank open wagon, complete with a very accurate chassis. The third range of value is Ratio, which produce excellent kits of the LNWR standard open and low-side wagons, again types which were used throughout the LMS years. Ratio also offer the LMS bogie ore wagon and standard box van and 3-plank wagon.

Among ready-to-run models, the old Airfix but now the present Dapol range includes the standard LMSR 20ton brake van and good models are produced by Mainline and Dapol of the standard LMS covered van and the 12ton open 5-plank wagon, though both these have the standard chassis again, which means that the brake gear is not entirely accurate.

Dapol have produced the SR covered 12ton van in correct LMSR livery, too, depicting the big batch of these which were purchased from the Southern railway. Mainline has made a

good likeness of the LMSR container for furniture removals and a Conflat. Neither of these models are 100% accurate, but they are correctly printed and capture the true LMS flavour.

When it comes to private owner (PO) wagons and such specialised type as tank wagons, the ready-to-run ranges should be approached with caution. They include many appropriate names for the LMSR area, but the excellent finish is often applied to models which are only approximately correct (again because standard mouldings are used) and any modeller not happy with this should check the model where possible from reference books before purchasing.

For 100% accuracy in PO liveries and types, look back to the Slaters' range of kits where the private owner colour schemes are not only correct but are applied to correct wagon types. The same can be said of the private owner wagon kits in the Cambrian range.

While we are on the subject of PO wagons, it is worth pointing out that before 1940 these were not operated as haphazardly as most modern modellers seem to think. Most operated on fairly fixed routes. The bulk of open PO wagons were used to ship coal, and they carried this from any given colliery to wherever the coal was contracted to be delivered. In a goods train there might well be a whole string of PO wagons from one colliery in the train – and all with different running numbers. Slaters recognise this and supply several alternative numbers with their kit transfer sheets. With other models you might need to alter the numbers by hand. Coal merchants' wagons also did not wander, as they came either from a colliery or coal distribution depot to the coal merchant's siding, and ran back when empty. Again, a layout could do with more than one the same, ensuring that the names chosen are believable for the right area – the name and the location printed on the wagons should make the choices self-evident. You are on easier ground for a post-1940 period layout, for PO wagons were 'pooled' from then until nationalization and the sort of haphazard mixes commonly seen on model layouts were indeed part of the scene.

The final observation concerns the question of just what freight stock you will need to obtain when building up an LMSR layout.

Above left:

This BISC ore wagon was another private owner type running on LMSR metals in the 1930s. Compare the prototype and the model included in the Mainline range. Note that while quite close to the original in this case, the model's chassis varies in detail because the model uses a standard chassis. Altering the model details will enhance its authenticity. *Ian Allan Library*

Left:

A detail that could provide a scenic touch in freight yards – putting ice through the roof hatches of insulated or refrigerated vans. Note the wagon on the left showing the unpainted interior, and the typical goods shed wood loading platforms. *Ian Allan Library*

Available kits and models provide a rich selection of prototypes, as we have seen, almost certainly all that a medium size LMS layout could absorb. But before starting to worry about it, bear in mind that not all the stock on LMS metals was owned by that operating company. Because of reciprocal agreements and the 'common user' agreements of the 'Big Four' there could be vans and wagons of all the railway companies in traffic.

Back in the 1970s the LMS Society interpreted LMS statistics for 1939 and worked out that there were 773 wagons for every 10 locomotives. Of the 773 just over half were private owner types and the rest were owned by the 'Big Four' companies, 166 by the LMS and the balance between the other three companies.

If you worked out this proportion per locomotive, you could arrive in rounded-off terms with eight wagons for every locomotive.

Above right:

Superb scratch-building by the Rev Peter Samuels produced this 4mm scale LMS standard open wagon (coupled to an old SR type), which is correct in every detail, in particular the chassis and brake gear. In pre-1936 grey finish, the model has the N markings to indicate 'non-common user' and the 'x' to indicate that it is fitted with through braking. *Brian Monaghan*

Right:

The standard LMS 12ton box van as produced by Mainline in 4mm scale, seen with the same type of van as sold to ICI and in that company's livery.

Below:

For maximum effect get several private owner wagons the same (but change the numbers). Here in July 1939 a whole string of City of Birmingham Gas Department coal wagons is going over the hump at the big Toton yard through which much LMSR coal traffic passed. *Ian Allan Library*

Above left:
LMSR gunpowder van is an attractive type based on the GWR 'Iron Mink' which could be adapted from the Ratio kit. *Ian Allan Library*

Above:
Standard LMS 13ton open goods wagon in pre-1936 finish. Note that weight details are on the LMS plate on the solebar, and only tare weight is painted on the side. Solebars are painted body colour, and all is black below solebar level, as are buffer heads and brake pipes. *Ian Allan Library*

Left:
Fitted vans which could run attached to passenger trains in special service – in this case for fish traffic – were painted in crimson lake and were fully lined out and lettered in the coaching stock style. Note data on solebars and the white star indicating brake reservoir. *Ian Allan Library*

Below:
Standard open containers on ex-LNWR low side goods wagons specially adapted and marked for container service. The LMS had many of these wagons. The scene is Ford's Dagenham factory with the pioneer Ford company diesel locomotive providing the motive power. *Ian Allan Library*

Of these four would be private owner (mainly coal or tank) wagons, one or two LMS and two or three from other 'Big Four' companies. Multiply these proportions as you need to suit your layout size, but with the allocation of model types as described you should get a realistic display of believable wagons on to your layout.

Some operating restrictions

If you have only a small layout, then the various restrictions on train lengths are hardly likely to worry you, but on large exhibition type layouts the knowledgable LMSR modeller, if tempted to run long trains, should bear in mind the following maximum lengths: Milk, parcels and carriages with horse boxes, 25 vehicles in each case; horse boxes and fish vans, 30 vehicles each (except the main fish working from Aberdeen – 40 vehicles from Carlisle, 35 south of Carlisle); empty bogie coaches, 20 vehicles; empty 6-wheel coaches or 4-wheel coaches, 30 vehicles; passenger train, 15 coaches (or not exceeding 500 tons maximum) except where authorised. Four-wheel vehicles with a wheelbase of 9ft or more could be worked on express passenger trains but had to be marshalled behind the coaches or next to the locomotive where the end position was not possible. By the late 1930s 4-wheel or

Above left:

Standard LMS 16ton steel mineral wagon, a forerunner of the better known BR type. This one is in the bauxite brown livery with post 1936 style of marking and pictured in 1945. The end and bottom door markings were perpetuated by BR. *Ian Allan Library*

Left:

Standard LMS meat container, of type BR. It is white with roof, trim, and lettering black. It is standing on the standard LMS container truck designed specifically to take this size container. The date is 1936, and the wagon is marked with the N to indicate that it is not common-user. *Ian Allan Library*

Below:

The LMS had many types of container. The FR type was for imported fruit or meat and was white with black root, trim, and lettering. Another rarely modelled item shown in this picture is the low rail mounted trolley used to move the container around in goods yards. This is a 1935 picture. *Ian Allan Library*

6-wheel coaches could still be used, but had to be mixed with bogie stock, always coupled to a bogie coach. Vehicles with a rigid wheelbase of 15ft or more could be marshalled anywhere in a passenger train so long as they had through brakes, and steam heat pipes. Open carriage trucks and fish trucks less than 21ft long could not be attached to passenger trains, nor could bogie freight vehicles or low side wagons even if fitted with through brakes. Six-wheel milk tankers could be attached to any passenger or milk train, but 4-wheel tankers could not be run at more than 60mph and had to have a bogie vehicle coupled behind. Maximum permitted tanker train length was 20 vehicles and no more than ten could be attached to a passenger train.

On a mixed train the freight wagons had to be marshalled behind the coaches and a brake van was to be provided. Mixed train maximum length was 30 wagons. One brake van had to be provided for every ten (10ton) or twenty (16ton) wagons on a mixed train. Where speed restrictions on a branch line were 25mph or less, all trains could run mixed. Locomotives, on special trains and excursions, were required to show a telegraphing number on the front which was usually on a small board on the smokebox door, often affixed to a lamp iron.

Right:
Container handling with an overhead yard crane suggests a model set-up which would really capture the LMSR atmosphere for the company did a busy trade in container traffic. This is a B type container of about 1927 seen in 1929-30. Of wood and painted grey with white letters, it was used for general cargo, but some of this type were specially fitted inside with racks for confectionery and biscuit traffic.
Ian Allan Library

Centre:
Stanier standard 60ft 3rd class open in 1938 showing the recently introduced black ends and solebars, plus end boards on the corridor connection and dark grey (instead of silver) roof. Note seat capacity marked on solebar.
Ian Allan Library

Bottom left:
Ex-LNWR coach, typical of many pre-group types in LMSR service, shown in a suburban train of mixed types at St Pancras.
Alan Whitehead

Bottom right:
Push-pull driving end detail. Note end marked 'PL & PH', though this was often spelled out in full. At Apsley Guise Halt on the Bedford-Bletchley line, steps were put down for passengers because of the ground level platform.
T. Rounthwaite

5 A Question of Colour

Inevitably the question of colour and finish affects all models, both in its intrinsic interest and variety, and in the pursuit of authenticity. It is certainly not sufficient to be satisfied with any model having 'LMS' on its side, and to accept it without question. Leaving aside the question of a model's authenticity as an LMSR type (dealt with in the previous chapter) the discerning modeller re-creating the LMS scene in miniature will want authentic colours and finish for the period of the layout.

For despite the relatively short life of the LMS there were a number of changes of finish and marking over that time span, and the unknowing modeller could easily make the mistake of running a locomotive in the style of 1946 (for example) on a layout purporting to depict the early 1930s. This will ruin any sense of authenticity which the layout tries to convey – and while some viewers might not spot the solecism, there will certainly be many who will.

Over the years there have been many books and articles dealing with aspects of LMSR liveries in great detail. These works should be studied for their very precise information, and for illustrations of examples. What follows here is a basic guide which will show the broad outline of the subject from a modelling aspect.

Locomotives

At the grouping in 1923, the new LMSR company, dominated as we have seen by ex-Midland Railway management in top appointments, adopted a colour scheme and finishing style almost identical to the smart and much admired Midland Railway style. Passenger locomotives were therefore painted in the rich red crimson-lake shade, which was applied to the superstructure sides and ends, and in some cases the cab roof or eaves. Black was applied to the smokebox, cab roof, and all horizontal surfaces such as the footplate and tank tops. Buffer beams and shanks were in the bright red shade of vermillion. The lining on splashers, tanks, tender sides etc, was black edging with a pale yellow ('straw') inside it. The boiler bands were not lined except for a black/yellow line behind the smokebox and immediately in front of the cab. There was much variation in lining depending on locomotive type, and the area to be lined out. For example wheels and cylinders were specified to be lined out, but this was not always done   or the lining was obscured by dirt.

Freight locomotives were black, unlined, and with plain vermillion buffer beams and shanks. The division into 'passenger' and 'freight' categories was somewhat arbitrary, so that '4F' 0-6-0s which were often used on passenger work, were always black, and some small tank engines which may have been used for pilot work were red. Initially, however, there were plenty of classes turned out in the red livery.

Numbers, in Midland style, were painted in 18in high gold leaf blocked letters on the centre of the tender side or tank side. On the cabside was the circular LMSR company crest, introduced from late 1923. Before this crest appeared the small letters 'LMS' were used in this position. On black freight locomotives the circular crest was rarely seen, and the letters 'LMS' or LMS inside a small vermillion panel were the usual markings. The lettering was gold, shaded red on passenger locomotives or plain gold on freight locomotives.

There was an inherent disadvantage in this method of numbering in that the occasional need to change tenders, when it took place, gave a locomotive an incorrect identity. In some cases this was overcome by painting the loco number in very small numbers on the cabside. There was also some opposition from within on the choice of the Midland style finish which was thought to look inappropriate on the old LNWR types, where a black lined-out livery was more familiar. Hence some LNWR locomotives remained in forms of LNWR livery for some years after 1923. In late 1927 came a change, presumably to overcome the tender problem. This put the letters LMS on the tender or tank side in place of the large number. The number was painted the same size on the cab side – and the standard height was 14in. There was some variation in letter and number size at first. Black freight locomotives had plain yellow (straw) numbering and lettering, while crimson lake locomotives had the gold style, shaded red. This livery was known as '1928 style'.

Two well-known 00 gauge model examples are the Lima Crab No 13000 which exhibits the original 1923 style passenger livery, with number on the tender, and the Hornby '2300' class 2-6-4T which exhibits accurately the 1928 style passenger finish.

By early 1928 the new livery style was being applied to all new locomotives coming in for repaint. Better flexibility was the aim, for the new system meant that tenders could be interchanged at will, thus ending the confusion sometimes seen when the locomotive and tender numbers did not match.

The crimson lake livery with its handsome lining was costly to apply, and needed a lot of cleaning. As economies were sought, it was decided to reduce the number of classes to which this LMS red finish was applied. Thus a new mixed traffic livery was introduced in 1928, black with single line red (vermilion) lining – simple but attractive. A gold, blocked red, lettering style was used with this livery, and the black was varnished, so giving a glossy finish when the locomotive was clean. Freight locomotives remained in plain black, and only the lettering and numbering was changed to the new styles and positions. In fact there was some variation in these black liveries. Some mixed traffic types were painted plain black without lining, particularly during the years of the depression, and

Left:
Though somewhat retouched, this photograph shows well the 1923 livery scheme for passenger locomotives, in this case as applied to the, as yet, unnamed No 6100, *Royal Scot* in 1927. Note lining on wheels, footplate, cylinders, and steps as well as on the superstructure. Large running number on tender side, crest on cab side, and smokebox cast number plate (but no shed plate as yet) can be seen. Also shown: loco number and company mark on lamps. *Real Photographs*

Left:
The 1923 livery for freight locomotives is illustrated on this 3F 'Jinty' No 16624 – plain black with straw yellow number and 'LMS' on a crimson lake panel, letters and outline also in yellow. No shed plate is affixed to this loco. *H. C. Casserley*

Centre left:
The 1928 style freight livery, also on a 'Jinty', with the number moved to the bunker side (cab side in tender locomotives) and the large LMS on the tank side, all straw yellow on varnished black. Power class (3F in this case), is painted high on the cab side. The diamond shape plate on the bunker is the builder plate of North British Loco Co who constructed this particular locomotive.

Bottom left:
A typical non-standard application of 1928 style livery to an ex-LNWR locomotive. Rebuilt 'Claughton' No 5953 *Buckingham* **has lettering in straw yellow, but the locomotive is plain black and the tender is still lined out in LNWR style (red/cream/grey lining). There is no smokebox number or shed plate, though the loco probably retained its LNWR shed plate on the rear of the cab roof.** *Ian Allan Library*

Top right:
The 1928 livery style for a passenger locomotive is seen on 'Royal Scot' class No 6147 *The Northamptonshire Regiment* **in 1929 with, in this case, the early style of plain unshaded lettering, probably hand-painted (later, transfers were used). Shaded blocked lettering was specified officially for locomotives in crimson lake livery. The coach illustrates the early style of finish with lined out panelling effect (even though this is a flush-side steel coach) with LMS and crest in the centre and the number at each end, all within the waist line.** *Ian Allan Library*

Centre right:
A 'Princess Coronation' class locomotive, No 6252 *City of Leicester,* **fitted with a streamlined tender, in the wartime austerity black livery with shaded style lettering. Power class is painted below number.** *British Rail*

Bottom right:
The final 1946 style livery for principal express engines; *City of Stoke-on-Trent* **demonstrates the 1946 'Block' lettering and the straw yellow and maroon lining on a black locomotive.** *British Rail*

lettering styles varied from gold shaded red to plain unblocked pale yellow (straw). From 1938 yellow replaced gold in the shaded style of lettering. As time went by, therefore, there was much variation. A lined out black locomotive might have unblocked yellow lettering rather than the specified gold-blocked style, and occasionally a plain black locomotive had blocked lettering. In the later 1930s also, the pale 'straw' lining was changed to brighter chrome yellow and lining of the wheels was discontinued on crimson lake engines. Also a style of lettering in gold with black shading was introduced as a variation on the red blocked style.

The crimson lake livery was eventually restricted to Pacifics, principal 4-6-0 types, some pre-grouping 4-6-0s and Midland Compounds. During the transition period to the new livery some smaller types also appeared in crimson lake for a time, among them the early '2300' class 2-6-4Ts and some station pilots and pre-grouping locomotives.

The lined black livery was applied to such types as the 2300 class 2-6-4Ts, Midland 2Ps, Stanier Class 5s, passenger tank engines and some Compounds from the late 1930s. In most cases all lettering was 14in high but spacing of LMS varied somewhat with the locomotive; 10in and 12in high lettering could also be used. It is interesting to note that when the LMSR took into service a number of diesel shunters in the mid-1930s, they conformed to the rule and were painted black with straw lettering and vermillion buffer beams to accord with their freight locomotive classification.

A large number of locomotives stayed in the 1928 style of finish until the end of the LMSR in 1948 – and afterwards. There are certainly recorded instances of a few locomotives still in crimson lake until 1951-52 – well into BR days. Also the pre-1928 livery style with the big tank or tender side numbers overlapped the 1938 style considerably in a few cases. Some engines carried this original style until World War 2 and at least one tank engine was still painted in the pre-1928 style as late as 1944. From the modeller's point of view, it can be seen that there is fair scope to overlap painting styles so long as this is not overdone.

In 1936 a new style of lettering and numbering was introduced – a sans-serif type to give a more 'modern' style. It was applied to relatively few engines, though, mainly new

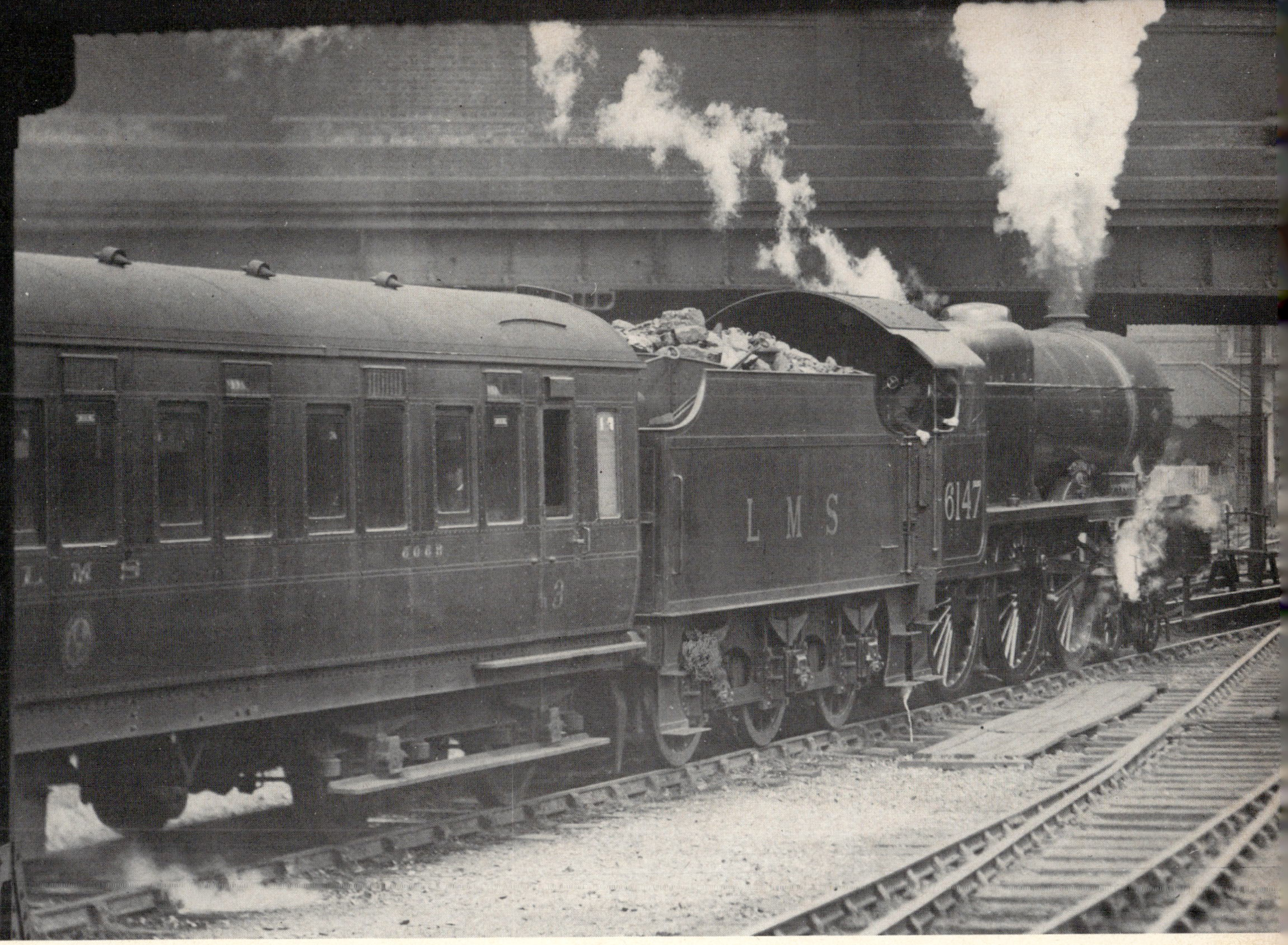
L M S
6147

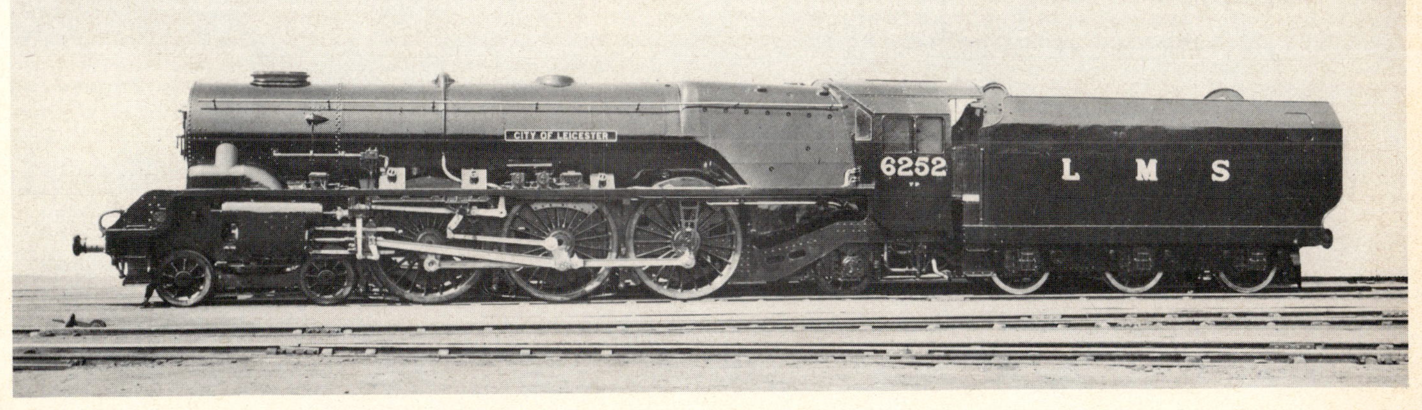

CITY OF LEICESTER
6252
L M S

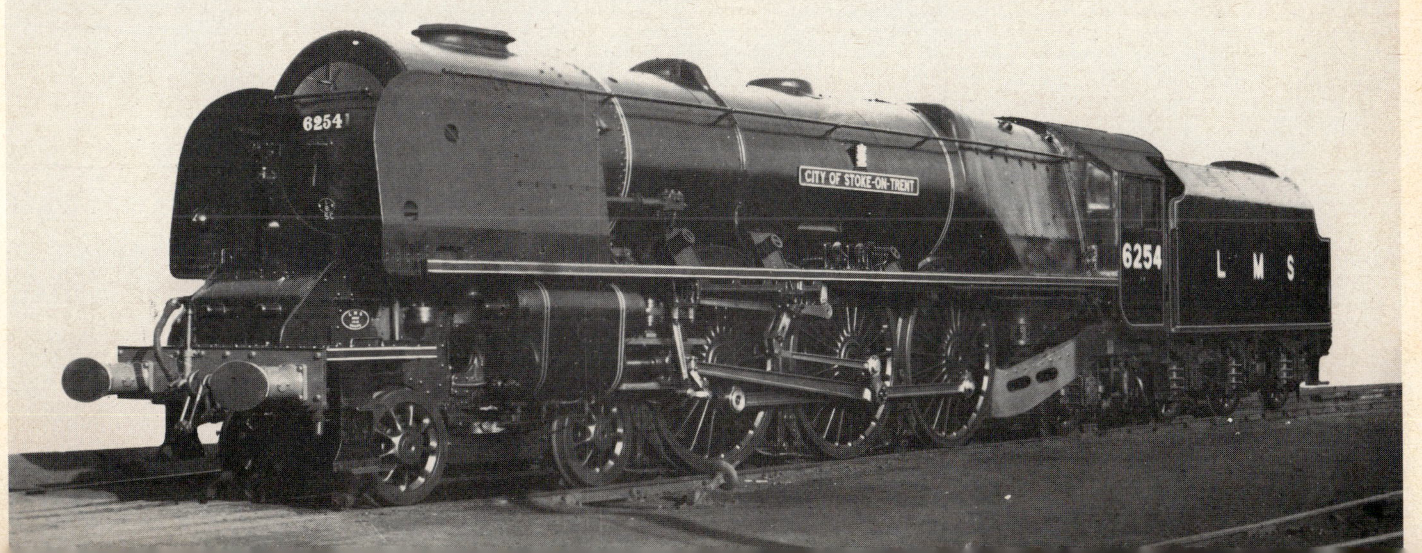

6254
CITY OF STOKE-ON-TRENT
6254
L M S

Right:
The early style of painting about 1930 when a panelled finish was given even to new flush-sided stock such as this brake end coach for principal expresses. Points to note: crimson lake ends, 'LMS' and number at opposite ends, crest in centre, the yellow end triangle indicating Midland lines restriction, 'LMS' on corridor end boards, black solebars and the crimson lake seemingly carried up to the rain strip with the roof silver-grey inside the rain strip area.
Ian Allan Library

Centre right:
Final style of coach painting on a Stanier brake/3rd. Note black ends, all silver-grey roof, yellow lining at cantrail, waist, and above windows, and maroon instead of crimson lake as the base colour. Grey panels for chalking instructions are painted on the brake end doors.
Ian Allan Library

Below:
An interesting comparison; the panelled coach on the left is in the post-1934 finish with horizontal yellow lining only, while the flush-sided coach at right is in the pre-1934 full panelled finish, simulating panelling. Photo dates from 1936.
Ian Allan Library

construction rather than repaints of existing engines. The sans-serif style of lettering had only a short life, however, and the company reverted to the seriffed style in 1940.

When the famous streamlined 'Princess Coronation' Pacifics appeared in the late 1930s they had new and distinctive liveries – red with gold 'speed' lines or blue with silver 'speed' lines. The coaches of their special trains were similarly painted.

Right from the start the LMSR specified that a cast number plate be carried on the smokebox door with a shed code plate below, again perpetuating an old Midland Railway practice. The MR did this to facilitate identification from the front in their 'round house' style engine sheds. In practice only ex-MR and new LMSR standard types *always* had these smokebox plates. Some other pre-group locomotives had them initially, but from 1928 the requirement was discontinued, but pre-group locomotives from other constituents allocated to ex-MR sheds often had them fitted. On ex-LNWR lines, also, white enamel LNWR style shed plates were retained, even for LMS standard types until 1935.

During World War 2 virtually all locomotives coming in for repair and repaint were turned out in plain black, including even the streamlined Pacifics. After World War 2 there was a time of severe austerity. Therefore plain black was applied to all locomotive types, but straw-yellow and lake lining was approved to go over the black on principal classes of Pacifics and 4-6-0s. A completely new lettering style, called 'Block' was

Above left:
A distinctive LMS type, the insulated milk van, which is a six-wheeler allowing it to run attached to passenger trains, and for this reason it is in crimson lake finish with shaded passenger-stock lettering, though the number is in plain freight-stock style lettering. Photograph taken, when new in July 1935. *Ian Allan Library*

Left:
Specially fitted and finished set for the 'Coronation Scot' of 1937. The colour is blue with silver lining. *Ian Allan Library*

Below:
LMS finish surviving in the BR age. Ex-LNWR, Webb 0-6-2T with a local train at Swansea Victoria station in March 1949. Like most ex-LNWR engines No 27625 lacks a smokebox number plate but it does have a standard LMS shed plate. The standard compartment stock is in LMSR maroon finish with the horizontal lining. *H. Daniel*

introduced, and this was in pale straw colour. This was applied to all new construction, but was quite rarely seen on older locomotives. Naturally, there were plenty of locomotives still to be seen in the 1928 style of finish up to 1948 and beyond, but from the modeller's point of view it is important to stress that the 'Block' style only applies from 1946 onwards. Thus a model locomotive with 'Block' lettering should accord with its period, and should not be on a layout set in the 1930s.

Coaching Stock

As with locomotives, so with coaches, and the Midland Railway colours were therefore standardised for the LMSR. For some time after the grouping, of course, the old pre-group colours of the constituent companies were still to be seen, particularly on some old coaches that were not worth repainting. As late as 1933, 10 years after the grouping, some coaches in LNWR and LYR livery were still in service. This is worth remembering for it gives a good excuse to include some colour variety in your coaching stock if your layout period is set in the early 1930s or before.

The MR colour used as the LMSR standard coach colour was crimson lake. This was continued round the ends and originally included solebars and underframes. From 1937, new coaches and old ones being repainted had black ends and black solebars and underframes, this being yet another economy measure. Pictorial evidence suggests that black solebars appeared earlier than this, however. In 1946 ordinary maroon paint, a

Top left:
The 1946 style 'Block' lettering applied to a Webb 2-4-2T which, in this 1949 view, has had a Block style '4' added in front of its LMSR number. Typical of ex-LNWR engines it lacks both smokebox number and shed plates. Loco is shunting at Aylesbury. *C. R. L. Coles*

Centre left:
The early style of LMS goods stock painting on a new ventilated goods wagon in November 1929. The grey is light, and the capacity is indicated only on the LMS plate on the solebar, the tare weight being also painted on the solebar. Note white brake handle, solebar in body colour, and other fittings black. White tyres were probably painted for this official picture as they are rarely seen in other pictures of this period.
Ian Allan Library

Left:
A patchy darker shade of grey is visible on this 12 ton coal wagon, compared with the lighter grey on the solebars and buffer beams, which probably indicates a repainted (with 'Smudge') vehicle. Number and tare weight are painted on side, and capacity is on the cast LMSR plate. The white stripe indicates end doors at the higher end of the stripe. Later the diagonal strap at the appropriate end was painted white instead.
Ian Allan Library

slightly darker shade, was substituted for crimson lake. Roofs were silver-grey or aluminium colour throughout the LMS period, but they were usually much darkened and dirtied by smoke and grime.

The lining out was in black with straw-yellow edging – gold edging is believed to have been used instead of yellow for coaching stock of principal trains. Originally, the lining was applied to all panel beadings in the old lavish pre-grouping style, and varied to suit the panelling of the coach. When the LMSR introduced modern flush-sided stock around 1930, the fully lined panel style was applied even though there were no panel beadings. This gave the effect of panelling even though it was completely dummy. This was somewhat absurd and expensive and to save time and money the whole lining-out scheme was simplified from early 1934 and horizontal lines were applied – a simple yellow line beneath the cantrail, and there was a line above the doors and windows and a double yellow line with a black centre was applied at the waist below the window level. In the later 1930s the yellow changed to a brighter chrome yellow from the old-style straw, and in 1946 changed back to a straw shade. Panelled coaches conformed to the new lining style, panels notwithstanding.

During World War 2 the lining was not always applied, and it was sometimes omitted after that from minor types like parcels vans or full brakes.

Originally the letters 'LMS' were placed in the centre waist panel with the numbers at each end in the waist panels, but from 1929 coach markings consisted of 'LMS' in the blocked seriffed style 6in high at the left end below waist level (when viewed from the side) and the running number in matching style at the right hand end. Special notations such as 'Sleeping Car', etc, when appropriate, were applied in the centre in line with the other markings. The numbers 1 or 3 (10in high) were applied to doors, also below the waist line. In the later 1930s a sans serif style lettering replaced the seriffed type, but from about 1940 the serif style was re-introduced. Naturally, all these styles were to be seen as time progressed because coaches were repainted over a long period. During the 1930s a circular LMS emblem was introduced and this was placed in the centre of all main line corridor coaches. It was put between the words 'Dining Car' etc, when these were carried, but in some cases it was put below them. Some pre-group coaches had coded symbols at the ends – for example a yellow triangle indicated that the coach could not be used on ex-Midland Railway lines (which had a restricted loading gauge). A yellow cross indicated a restriction on both the Midland and Maryport & Carlisle Railway lines.

Ready-to-run coaches which are authentic LMSR replicas are all in correct livery as sold. Kit-built models must be painted to the required period styles. Transfers for all periods are readily available and some examples are shown in the photographs.

Structures

A firm record of colours used on all buildings in LMSR days is hard to find, and surviving reports state that, in the 1930s at any rate, new structures were made in contemporary materials, and woodwork and trim was sometimes coloured to suit. The 'official' colours for larger areas of woodwork on stations and signalboxes were light stone (BS 361), and adjacent panelling, guttering, drainpipes, framing, steps, and valancing was brown (BS 412). Noticeboards and signposts had black lettering on white or cream backgrounds and station nameboards had black lettering on a pale yellow background. The light stone as specified was of a 'dark' shade rather than the light shade the name suggests.

Woodwork on some of the modern buildings (doors, window frames etc,) put up in the 1930s has been recorded as emerald green, bright blue, etc, despite the fact that the 'official' general colour was supposed to be brown.

Freight Stock

As with coaching stock, the basic Midland Railway scheme and livery was adopted as the LMSR standard for freight stock. This was grey, though it came in more than one shade. The official shade was a quite light grey, but the MR (and LMSR) had the practice of mixing old paint stocks (known as 'smudge') for use on repainted or refurbished wagons, and this was invariably darker than the 'new' shade, and furthermore could differ from batch to batch depending on the mix.

In 1929 the company issued new paint mix instructions which used more black, and from that time on the grey was noticeably darker, the shade that most enthusiasts would consider as 'LMS grey'. Though the main model paint makers all issue shades of grey labelled as LMS, Midland, etc, which are acceptable, it is

Top left:
Block trains are nothing new – the LMS was running them from 1929 using this type of side-discharge 40ton hopper to carry coal from Toton to Stonebridge Park power station which provided the company's electricity in the London area. *Locomotive Publishing Co*

Centre:
The 1936 goods stock livery is portrayed here. This standard 12ton shock absorbing wagon is in bauxite brown. It carries the small LMS letters, its capacity, its tare weight, and 'N' for 'non-common user' all in the prescribed positions. As a special purpose wagon it also carries its telegraphic code SAW. The three white stripes were a 'shunt with care' warning and they were later applied at the ends as well – they were only painted on this type of wagon.
National Railway Museum, York

Left:
The austerity finish used in World War 2 and up to nationalisation. The woodwork was left bare except for areas which carried lettering. Top is a standard 13ton open merchandise wagon, and below a low-side open wagon of the engineering department (E), for the Stoke depot.
National Railway Museum, York

Left:
Bulk grain van in 1935 in the standard grey finish, and with its capacity and tare weight marked on the body but the telegraphic code (BGV) on a plate on the solebar.
National Railway Museum, York

Below left:
United Dairies tank wagon, showing solebar markings when new about 1929. Milk tank wagons were built as six-wheelers from about 1937, allowing them to run attached to passenger trains if necessary.   *Locomotive Publishing Co*

There was a major change from May 1936 when the colour of freight vehicles was altered to bauxite brown, and the large LMS lettering was replaced by small 'LMS' 4in high letters above the number and weight capacity. Vacuum-fitted wagons were now marked XP instead of X and this code in 4in letters appeared above the wheelbase which was now also painted at the right hand corner of the body. The wheelbase was indicated in feet and inches, thus:

$$WB - 9' - 6''$$

Where the wagon had a code name (eg, Parrot), this was painted on the solebar or lower body edge. Tarpaulins for wagons were of black canvas, clearly marked in white with LMS and a number showing out to each side.

In 1936 some grey vehicles were finished in the newer style of small lettering, and the pre-1936 style with big 'LMS' letters was still to be seen for the rest of the LMSR lifetime and could still be encountered well into BR days. In World War 2, lettering was often reduced to a smaller size, and wagons were unpainted (left in bare wood) except for the number panels which were painted as a background for the markings.

The LMSR had many containers and these were variously painted and lettered according to type. Open top containers were grey (or bauxite from 1936) lettered like wagons. Closed containers were either white with black lettering (and black ironwork where applicable) or crimson lake with yellow lettering, sometimes in coaching stock style. Containers for special traffic (eg, removals service) were usually marked with advertising panels for the service.

Road Vehicles

Ordinary horse-drawn drays or lorries (of which the LMSR had many) were painted dark grey (officially 'lead') with white LMS lettering and numbers similar in style to wagon application.

Horse-drawn parcels vans were crimson lake, as were motor vans, all lettered rather ornately in passenger stock style, and other non-parcels service vehicles were lake with cream or straw yellow lettering. Mudguards and chassis were black. During World War 2 white edging was applied to all mudguards. Buses followed the passenger stock style of crimson lake with the more elaborate seriffed lettering. In the 1920s quite ornate lining out was applied to some of the road vehicles.

equally in order for the modeller not to be too pedantic about the resulting shade because it varied in real life.

The grey was carried over the solebars, but all below that, plus couplings, buffers, shanks, and brake levers, was black. Brake lever handles were white. Interiors of vans and open wagons were usually not painted at all, but brake vans were painted light green internally with a white ceiling. Roof tops were specified to be the same colour as coach roofs – aluminium (silver-grey), but in practice they ended up dirty dark grey from the smoke and weathering.

All rolling stock was marked on the centre of the side with a white 'LMS' in the largest size, to fit the depth. On a coal wagon the letters were of the largest size, 18in deep. On a flat truck, obviously, the letters were very much smaller, as small as 4in in depth.

The running number was painted in 4in high white numbers, applied at the lower left corner (viewed from the side). On some brake vans the number was 5½in high inside a white-outlined black panel positioned centrally. This was the original Midland practice, and not all brake vans carried the number here. Many brake vans of non-Midland origin had the number positioned as for ordinary wagons.

The capacity in tons was originally carried only on the cast number plate which every vehicle had on the solebar. Very soon after grouping, however, the weight expressed in tons (T for short, eg: 12T) was painted above or adjacent to the running number in 3in high letters. Sometimes 'TONS' was printed in full. The tare weight was painted in figures for tons-cwt-quarters (thus 12-2-3) on the lower right corner of the side. On brake vans it was given in tons only with 'T' or 'Tons' spelled out.

Stock which was not 'common user' was marked with a white 'N' 4in high at the lower corners of the sides as far outwards as they could go. Vacuum-braked stock all carried a 12in high 'X' on the side, and a white star was usually marked by the brake pipe itself.

6 On the Lineside

Because the LMS inherited so much from its constituent pre-group companies there was little need to plan immediate replacement of equipment such as signals, trackside signs, signalboxes, stations, and so on. Therefore the common 'style' which was characteristic of the GWR never developed to the same degree as the LMSR.

Instead, all areas retained the equipment and structures of the original companies and in many cases these outlived the LMSR and survived well into the BR period – even to the present time. Thus the LNWR style of standardised station structure did not disappear in favour of an LMS design, and examples abounded in every part of the system of pre-grouping fittings. In some areas no single item of LMSR equipment ever appeared on the scene.

From the modeller's point of view, therefore, it is essential to define the area and period of your layout, for even some common items of LMSR equipment did not appear for some years after the LMS was formed. Care is needed to avoid solecisms. For example, if your layout was set around 1930 and you installed the readily available Ratio LMSR tubular post signals, you would be very wrong, for this type of standard item was not introduced until 1935! As ever some close research is needed on your particular area of work before you begin, so that errors like this are avoided.

Signals

Taking signals first, all the pre-group types were perpetuated until replacements were needed. Standard designs were developed for semaphore arms, lights, ladders, and posts, but in the meantime old pre-group stocks were used up. What is now thought of as the classic tubular post signal of the LMSR, was introduced, initially with a wood post quite similar to a design which the LNWR had built.

The wood gave way to the steel tubular post in 1935, though lattice was used for signal posts higher than 30ft. As an economy measure this rule was soon modified to allow the post to be 35ft high to do away with the need for lattice. Excellent 4mm scale models of the LMSR tubular signals (home and distant) are included in the Ratio range, but cast kits in N, 00, and 0 have been produced by small specialist firms at various times.

Bracket and gantry signals usually had the signal posts of the tubular variety on a gantry or bracket which could be made of lattice or squared off wood posts. There was much mixing of old components also. Thus it was possible to find LNWR wood posts fitted with standard signal arms and ladders. The LMS signal arm of 1935 onwards was a simple flat metal pressing known as the Nicholls pattern after its maker.

Below:
Rhosneigr, an old LNWR station that survived into BR days, but when photographed in 1950 was still in LMS condition and with paintwork in brown and stone. *British Rail*

Bottom right:
Warmley station, ex-MR, in 1946, with woodwork in stone and brown, which is also probably the colour of the MR plate girder bridge in the foreground. Note also the valancing on the canopy which would also be brown. *R. E. Read*

Below:
Bedford St Johns station showing LMSR and Southern timetable boards, LMSR porter's trolley, brown and stone paintwork, and the nameboard (far right) with black letters on pale yellow background. *V. R. Anderson*

On Midland lines the old Midland Railway standard design was perpetuated. This had a corrugated lower quadrant arm, and wood post of square cross-section, all topped by a handsome finial. The basic design was adopted by the new company as a standard type at the grouping. From 1925 the finial was discarded in favour of a flat top piece, and some later fittings were subsequently installed. The modified Midland type signal was still being installed during the early 1930s until the new standard design, already mentioned, replaced it.

Two important details you may wish to add to signals of the LMSR period are a white diamond on the post to indicate track circuiting, and a 'D' to indicate a 'callbox' on the signal from which the signalbox could be contacted. Signal posts were white with black bottom sections, and there was a black section behind the white diamond where this was fitted.

The LMSR was in the forefront of colour light signalling and copied one or two ideas and procedures from America. First colour light signals were a direct semaphore replacement on the Bow Road-Barking route in 1926. They were two-aspect only. In 1929 the Manchester Victoria area had four-aspect light signals installed, and during the 1930s the four-aspect system was extended to several main routes, including the Euston-Watford and the Glasgow area. There was also a three-aspect dwarf light signal for placing between the tracks in the '6ft way'.

Signalboxes

As with signals, so with signalboxes. Initially, local pre-group designs were repeated, sometimes in slightly less decorative form. First steps in standardisation came with the decision to use the LNWR standard design for the Central and Western Divisions of the LMSR and the Midland standard design for the Eastern Division plus the Crewe area. The Caledonian design was used in Scotland. This arrangement stayed in force until 1927. The old Midland design was then modified (in effect combined with aspects of the LNWR design) to become the new standard type, with the first of these being erected in 1929. The new design had the distinctive Midland style cabin section, but without the rounded upper corners to the windows, and a brick lower section, LNWR style, in place of the Midland

Above left:
LMS spartan; Cold Meece in Staffordshire was built in wartime and is a stark and simple brick structure. *A. Cox*

Left:
One of relatively few new LMSR stations built. Elm Park is in the typical 1930s 'art deco' style and looked most attractive when new, being designed to suit the site. *British Rail*

Below left:
The Elm Park platform when new in 1935. Paintwork may be brown and stone but could be locally chosen colours. Nameboard is a rendering of the LMS 'Hawkseye' shape, though it is not an actual 'Hawkseye' product. The combination of seat and nameboard was a standard LMS design and was found at other new and modernised stations dating from the mid to late 1930s. *Ian Allan Library*

Below:
Luton station about 1945, with standard LMS concrete lamp standards. *Ian Allan Library*

wood construction. The roof was also of LNWR style, displacing the elegant hipped roof of the old Midland design. The Midland wooden ladder was retained but this was later replaced by a tubular steel staircase. The Dapol Midland signalbox kit is an obvious starting point for all LMSR signalbox models.

Also in the later 1930s, a number of very modern reinforced concrete signalbox were built in the then fashionable stark and functional style with flat roof and flared sides.

Stations and structures

Much less easy to define is a 'standard' LMSR station. Very little was done in the way of station building after grouping. Those few new stations which were opened were built to suit the site and though the 'modern' style was used with typical 1930s embellishments, there does not seem to have been a consistent pattern. Apsley station near Hemel Hempstead is a classic example of a stark modern station of the late 1930s. It has a ribbed concrete platform facing, with pre-cast panels which was standard, however, for it was to be seen on all new platform work.

Standard LMSR platform fittings included a reinforced concrete lamp post in single (inverted 'L') and double ('T') forms, introduced in the late 1930s, a functional wood seat for platforms, and the famous 'Hawkseye' nameboard, which was thoroughly standardised and was found on many stations. The old Midland fencing (from Ratio in 4mm scale) became the standard fencing on the LMSR.

There was also a standard platelayer's hut of plain brick, looking stark and not very homely. Outside toilets, cycle sheds and coal sheds were also produced to standard design and quite a number of asbestos sheds in goods yards (to act as provender stores or tool stores, etc) were erected. There was nominally a standard type as far as panels were concerned, but sizes varied with site and details changed from builder to builder. The Ratio provender store kit captures the look, though it is not a model of the LMS type. It is a BR pattern version which was not too dissimilar to huts of this sort put up in LMS days.

Gradient posts and mile posts were of standard types, all cast in concrete and with letters cast on. LMSR colours of these were white with black letters. The milepost, in particular, had a distinctive shape with an angled top displaying the figures. Cast models of some of these small items are to be found among the ranges of specialised makers, and it is also worth recalling that Ratio offers a 4mm scale LMS/GWR pattern loading gauge.

Road vehicles

In 1923 the company took over thousands of horse-drawn drays and lorries from the constituent companies, so many varied types of vehicle were to be seen in LMSR livery for most of its existence, as horse-drawn transport had not entirely disappeared even in 1948. Like other equipment the Midland type was continued in production as a stop-gap, but some standard designs rated at various tonnages were produced by the company, mostly single horse or pair-horse vehicles. Drawings and details of all these types are

included in the book *LMS Road Vehicles* (OPC) listed in the appendix. From the modeller's point of view there are several kits, some nonedescript, some specific, of horse-drawn vehicles which can be altered or detailed to LMS type. For example Slaters make kits for a horse-drawn parcels van in 4mm and 7mm scale which has a LMS 'look' about them but is not specifically LMS. Langley Miniature Models is another firm offering horse-drawn vehicle kits.

The motor vehicles included common makes of single-deck buses and coaches including the Leyland Lion, Leyland Tiger, AEC Regal, and various Albions. Kits to 4mm scale of some of these are to be had, and, again, reference pictures show the details peculiar to LMS vehicles. The LMS used motor vans and lorries similar to those sold commercially elsewhere throughout the period. Hence the AEC, Albion, Karrier, Leyland, Dennis, Austin, Fordson, Morris-Commercial and others can be used on a

Above:
LNWR standard ground signals. *British Rail*

Left:
LMS standard ground signals. *British Rail*

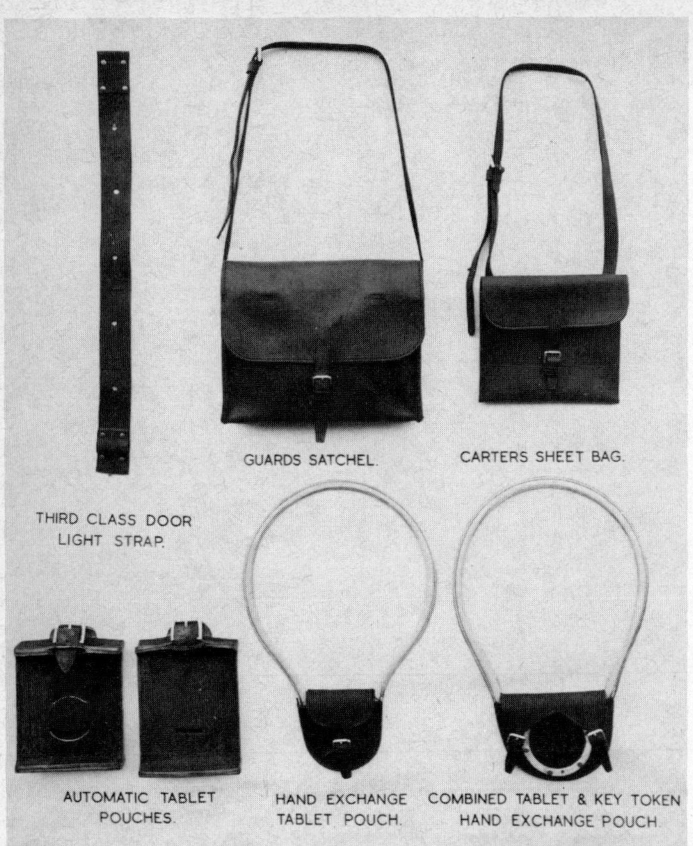

Above:
Standard LMS items in 1943, made to austerity standards with re-cycled material.
Ian Allan Library

Top right:
Tablet catching equipment, in operation on the Midland and Great Northern section of the LMS.
H. N. James

Above right:
LNWR standard station buildings were very much part of the LMSR scene and very many, such as Chester Road, remain in the modern BR era. *Arthur North*

layout depending on period and model. Anbrico Scale Models produce a 4mm scale white metal kit of a Dennis 2ton platform lorry, based on the LMS type and this is excellent in every respect. There are other 4mm and 7mm scale kits or models which can be adapted, though there is very little specifically produced in LMS form. The most characteristic railway vehicle of the 1930s and 1940s is, perhaps, the mechanical horse. Langley and others have made kits of these at various times. One of the pictures shows a Scammell Mechanical Horse of the 6ton type converted by the author some years ago from the old Airfix plastic kit of a BR period Scammel Scarab. This required a new flat nose and a curved roof made from plastic card, and proved to be a simple adaptation. The same conversion can be done with the current Merit kit of a Scammell Scarab in 4mm scale. A die-cast model of an LMSR Morris-Commercial parcels van is produced by Lledo in their 'Days Gone' range, but unfortunately is not to a model railway scale.

Left:
**Arthur North's plastic card model of a standard
LNWR station building, being made for his
LMSR period gauge 1 layout.**   *Arthur North*

Below left:
**Bill Hudson has caught the LMSR atmosphere on
ex-Midland lines with his 00 gauge layout. Here
is Ashover station, a typical Midland Railway
station building in Derbyshire, and with all stock
applicable to the 1928 period.**   *Brian Monaghan*

Above and right:
**Perfect LNWR atmosphere (in LMS days) is
caught on this 00 gauge layout where all
structures are based on actual LNWR survivors.**

Below right:
**Scammell Mechanical Horse converted from the
old Airfix BR Scarab version. Cab shape is
altered with plastic card. Finish is 1946 period.**

Limestone traffic on Bill Hudson's LMSR layout set on Midland lines in Derbyshire. Note how the Clay Cross hoppers have all been given different numbers. An elderly Johnson 3F with original boiler is the motive power. *Brian Monaghan*

Below:
Standard Midland Railway milepost, used in LMS era. *Arthur North*

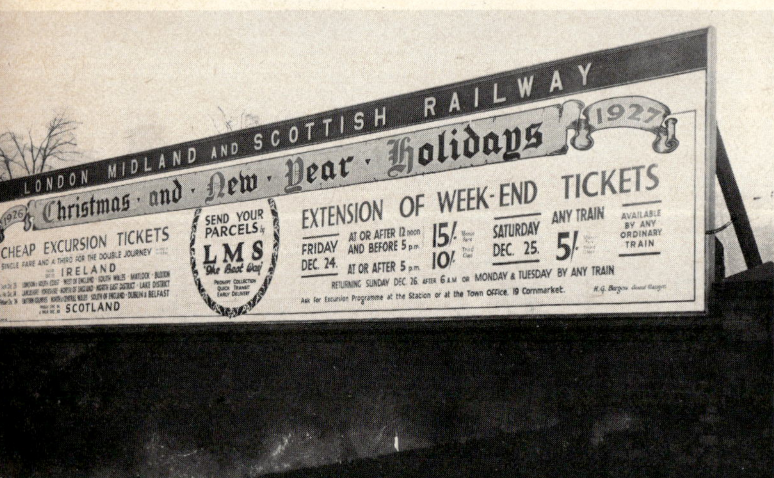

Above:
LMS poster hoarding with typical style of travel poster, in this case the end of year arrangements for 1926-27. Trains ran on Christmas Day then.
Author's collection

Above right:
The Midland Railway favoured roundhouse style locomotive sheds. This is Derby No 4 shed in 1910. *British Rail*

Right:
Other constituent companies preferred through engine sheds. A good small prototype which could handle large engines was Kyle of Lochalsh, a small but attractive two-road structure which lends itself to model making. All locomotives visible are Stanier 'Black Fives'. *A. W. Martin*

7 Making a start with modelling

As is self-evident from the contents of this book, there is certainly no shortage of good accurate models and kits available for the LMSR modeller although they are less well advertised, than the equivalent models produced for GWR enthusiasts, but much is available if you care to seek it out. If you are prepared to do a little repainting and detailing of ready-to-run models, and take care to get colour schemes accurate to the period you wish to model, you can come up with some effective modelling which will capture the true LMS character.

A few pointers are in order for those who, having read this book, wish to get on and start a LMSR layout or model collection.

To summarise, the N gauge enthusiast is better served for LMS models than any other sort save, perhaps, modern BR. There are the three Hornby-Minitrix steam locomotives – 2-6-2T, 2-6-0, and Fowler 0-6-0T dock tank which are among the best performers in this gauge. At the time of writing, however, these models had only ever been available in BR finish, so the LMS modeller will need to repaint these to period. Graham Farish offer a

Class 5, Midland Compound, and a 'Duchess', plus a BR diesel shunter which might be convertible to a closer resemblance to an early LMS diesel shunter. Then Gem offer bodyline kits for several other types which fit the Farish chassis, and there are a few other kits to be had such as a diminutive but accurate Sentinel shunter (to fit a Farish power bogie) from P & D Marsh. All this motive power together offers more than the average modeller could afford, or would need, so don't overlook N gauge for it is very much suited to LMS modelling.

The other popular size for the average modeller, 4mm scale, has even more to offer. Apart from many cast metal locomotive and rolling stock kits, the ready-to-run ranges offer nearly everything you would need. Standard coaches, brake vans, and some wagons are available almost literally 'off the shelf', so you can get into LMS modelling straight away. If you wonder which locomotives to invest in, start with two of the most accurate models made, the Hornby '2300' class Fowler 2-6-4T and the Airfix/Mainline Fowler '4F' 0-6-0. Both of these are good as they come, but could do with the usual weathering and blackening of wheels and motion, etc. You can further detail them in the manner shown in the accompanying pictures. The '4F' needs its piston tail rod covers removed from the buffer beam if your layout depicts a period later than

Top left:
One of the early LMSR diesel shunters pushing wagons over the hump at Toton yard in 1939. Note the colour light signal on the tubular post, and the typical ferro-concrete 1930s style control cabin. *British Rail*

Top right:
There was no shortage of small prototypes on the LMSR. This is Redditch coaling stage which would be a perfect prototype structure for a small layout. *R. Essery*

Above left:
Holywell Junction, an imposing LNWR structure with push-pull train for Holywell Town in bay platform. *H. D. Bowtell*

Above right:
Another small prototype with lots of character. This is Brondesbury Park station which is on an overbridge with steps down to the platform. *British Rail*

about 1937, and it can have tender coal rails added, and even a tender cab. Though this can be made from plastic card easily enough, an inexpensive etched kit for the tender cab is available from the Perseverance range produced by Kemp Models. This same range offers excellent conversion kits for the '2300' class, consisting of etched brass side overlays to produce a later production Fowler type or the final type with Stanier side-window cab.

Above:
A delightful prototype station for a branch line layout. This is Portpatrick, a branch from Stranraer. In pre-group days it was jointly owned by GSWR, CR, MR, and LNWR. Locomotive here is a 'Jumbo' 0-6-0 (ex-Caledonian Railway). The simple track layout can be seen in the picture and could be compressed slightly in length for a model layout. *British Rail*

Left:
First of the LMS 7120 series diesel shunters of 1944-46 vintage. It can be modelled easily from existing BR diesel shunter models, as shown in this book. *Ian Allan Library*

Above:
Into a new era. The pioneer LMS diesels, pull out of Euston with an express and start the main line diesel era. Nos 10000 and 10001 are black with a silver stripe and chrome cut-out lettering. Bogies are silver. Date is early 1948 just after nationalisation. *Ian Allan Library*

Both these models can therefore take on quite new character far removed from their 'stock' ready-to-run appearance, and the work is within the province of the beginner.

This is a good time to say that the LMSR is a friend to anyone with little painting skill. You can get away with plain black locomotives (even many mixed traffic types were devoid of the lining they should in theory have carried) and the plain yellow markings are as easy as any transfers to apply – the Kingprint (dry) transfer range, SMS, and PC, all include LMS letters and numbers. The fully lined out crimson lake LMS livery is admittedly difficult to apply without skill, but in practice the less-than-perfect painter can restrict conversion and repainting work to the lowlier black locomotives while acquiring the best of the other LMS ready-to-run types which were in crimson, from the Mainline and Hornby ranges. Such types as the 'Duchess', 'Jubilee', 'Patriot' and 'Royal Scot' have been done well in 4mm scale, notably the Mainline versions, with little extra work necessary to give you a perfect looking crimson finish locomotive. Wagons, signals, structures, and the like are all simply painted, too, with no complicated colour schemes to worry about.

To round off these ideas for making a start, bear in mind that sufficient lineside accessories are produced to give an immediate LMS flavour to any small layout – Ratio make LMS standard signals for 00 and N, plus the fencing, plus a GWR/LMS loading gauge, and LMS fencing. Some of the smaller firms offer LMS (or pre-group constituent) lamps and other station fittings. Dapol have a 4mm scale Midland signalbox which yields window sections and parts for conversions if you want to do more than use it as it comes.

For passenger stock a brake/3rd and compo from the Mainline range of LMS types give you an 'instant' and authentic short train, or there are the Midland and LNWR coach kits from Ratio. Farish have some freelance (but LMS/Midland style) compartment and 4-wheel stock for N gauge.

Brake van, private owner, and basic LMS wagons and vans are similarly easy to furnish from ranges such as Dapol and Mainline in 00 gauge, and Farish and Peco in N.

Some layout ideas
There is no question, therefore, that even a beginner to the hobby can get going straight away as a modeller of the LMS scene, using any of the particular models recommended above. Building a LMS layout – any layout come to that – is a more variable personal matter for its extent depends on your own circumstances of time, money, space and skill. The more experienced modeller will not lack ideas, and the model railway press carries many layout plans. For relative beginners simple layouts are commended, and there were plenty of pleasing branch lines and areas of the LMS which make an interesting basis for a layout. Among them are the Dursley branch (ex-Midland), St Albans (ex-LNWR), Burnham-on-Sea (Somerset & Dorset), Killin & Loch Tay (ex-Caledonian), Settle & Carlisle route (ex-MR), and Kyle of Lochalsh (ex-Highland). To give you further ideas, here are three very simple track plans, all based on actual locations which will enable authentic, if fairly basic, layouts to be built in small areas. Each could be expanded later, or you can keep them simple if, say, the LMS was a secondary interest and you wanted a suitable setting on which to display LMS models.

1 Dyserth

This branch (actually the Dyserth Light Railway) was built in the later half of the 19th century to serve the villages and limestone mines inland from Prestatyn, North Wales. It was owned by the LNWR. The plan features only Dyserth, the very tiny terminus, and it all fits in a minimum size of 6ft × 1ft 6in in 00 gauge using sectional or flexible track with small radius turnouts. The branch survived for limestone traffic until 1973, though passenger traffic ceased in the 1930s. If you have more length available use it to incorporate a fiddle yard. The service was intensive for a branch line in the 1930s and all trains were pushed from the junction because there were no run-around loops. There were no station platforms either, all being ground level affairs in American style. Originally railmotors were used for passenger service in LNWR days, then a 0-4-4T and push-pull coach in LMS days. Goods trains were short, often no more than three wagons and a brake van. There were no signals (one engine in steam working) except at the junction end, and no signal-boxes. All points were hand-thrown. This is ideal for a very simple LMS period model, more so because big locomotives were used with ample coal and water capacity, as the line had no water or coaling facilities either. In LMS days even 'Jubilee' or 'Patriot' class locomotives could be seen working the branch on occasion, though a '4F', Black Five, or a 2-6-4T were more usual. This type of layout works well. The author made a fictional station on this branch as an exercise in EM modelling, and it has proved to be a highly satisfying portable layout.

Below:
Dyserth branch – branch terminus at Dyserth.

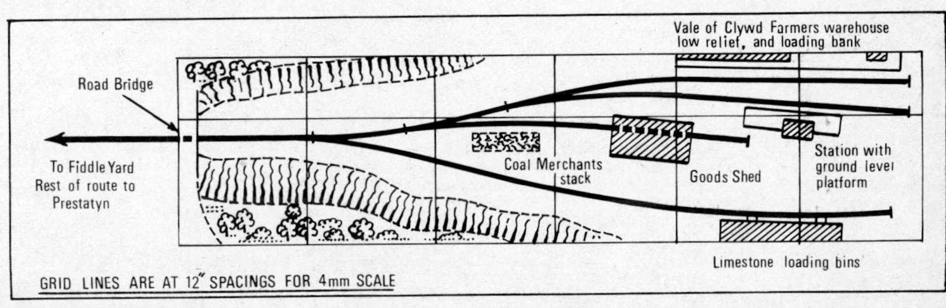

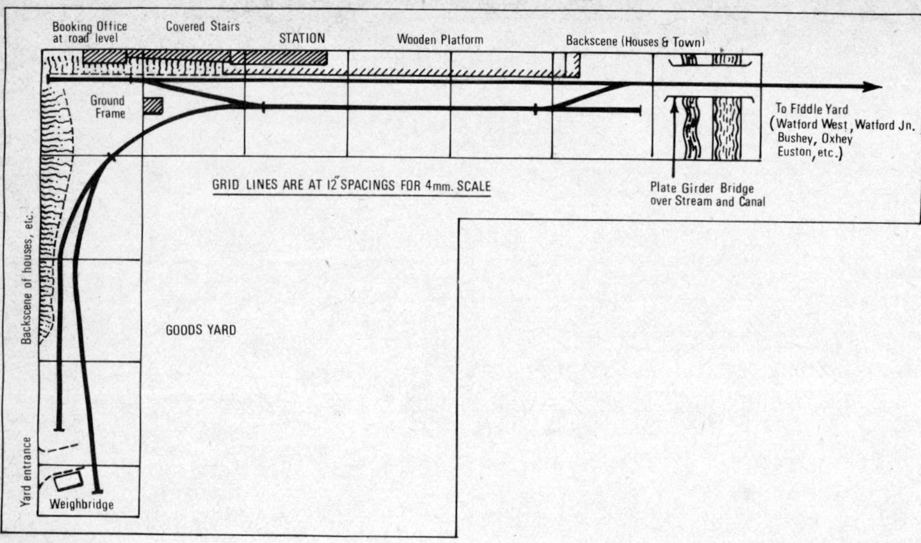

Above:
Croxley Green

2 Croxley Green

Croxley Green was one of several branch lines in the Watford area built by the LNWR when Watford was rapidly expanding as a centre for commerce and light industry, with a related population explosion. It was actually electrified in LNWR days and now the station survives as part of London Transport, although it was LMS until 1948, complete with its goods yard. Strictly speaking if you made a genuine Croxley Green layout in LMS days you would need 'Oerlikon' electric stock for the passenger service, but if you regard your version as a freelance layout based on fact, then there would be nothing to stop you using steam, such as the Fowler '2300' 2-6-4T with a couple of suburban coaches. The unusual shape of the real thing – making it ideal for a shelf layout fitting the corner of a room – was dictated by the site, for a main road runs parallel to the goods sidings, and the road was there first. So the LNWR bent the goods yard round at right angles using a very tight curve. Local freight and coal merchant's traffic was handled in the goods yard.

For a beginner this is a very good layout. Like the other two layouts suggested here it can be built using either sectional track or flex-track or a combination of the two. Shunting the yard is tricky – you can easily get snarled up – so this is a more interesting layout to operate than many other simple branch termini. The station platform in LMS days was a wood structure and in model form it could be made realistically by splicing about three Wills halt kits together. As the Croxley Green area is essentially residential, a backscene of 1920s and 1930s houses would be in order, and would effectively capture the suburban atmosphere.

3 Foxfield

If you prefer a busy junction, but with a simple track plan to fit 8ft × 4ft, this ex-Furness Railway location is interesting. It is adapted from an idea in Edward Beal's famous book of the past *Modelling the Old-Time Railways* (out of print). Trains from Foxfield ran to Barrow and Whitehaven on the main line, with a connecting branch to Coniston. Thus, this layout gives a chance to use 4-6-0s and quite short 'semi-fast' sets, plus a traditional style branch train set. Coniston branch trains used the platform road opposite the engine shed side, requiring 'wrong road' working. Obviously this plan, for continuous running with a storage loop, is compressed and simplified, but the character can be nicely reproduced and there is the charm of a small engine shed, and the unusual island platform with passenger access across the tracks. Though the plan shows a goods-shed, this was actually demolished quite early on. There was no footbridge to the platform.

The main line was actually double track at the real Foxfield, but to fit the layout into a space as small as 8ft × 4ft it has to be single track. From the beginner's point of view it is a good project, closely based on the real thing, though the station has been shown as a mirror reverse so as to make best use of the space. The baseboard, it is suggested, can be made up of two 4ft × 2ft end sections and two 4ft × 1ft centre sections, leaving a centre operating space of 4ft × 2ft. This helps your economics, for three Sundeala Hobbyboards or three softboard standard panels will yield the baseboard surface if the third panel is sawn lengthwise.

Appendix

Books for further reference
While there are very many books dealing with aspects of the LMS, the following titles (which are not necessarily always in print) are of particular reference value to modellers.

Salute to the LMS, Cecil J. Allen (Ian Allan)
LMS Album (Vols I-III), B. Stephenson (Ian Allan)
Locomotive Liveries of the LMS, D. Jenkinson/R. Essery (Roundhouse/Ian Allan)
Liveries of the LMS, Brian Haresnape (Ian Allan)
Fowler Locomotives, Brian Haresnape (Ian Allan)
Stanier Locomotives, Brian Haresnape (Ian Allan)
Ivatt & Riddles Locomotives, Brian Haresnape (Ian Allan)
LMS Road Vehicles, H. N. Twells/T. W. Bourne (Oxford Publishing Co)
LMS Wagons, Vols I, II, R. Essery (Oxford Publishing Co)
LMS Architecture, V. Anderson (Oxford Publishing Co)
Portrait of the LMS, D. Jenkinson/V. Anderson/R. Essery (Peco)
LMS Coaches, D. Jenkinson (Oxford Publishing Co)

Below:
Layout suitable for a bigger space, based on Foxfield Junction.

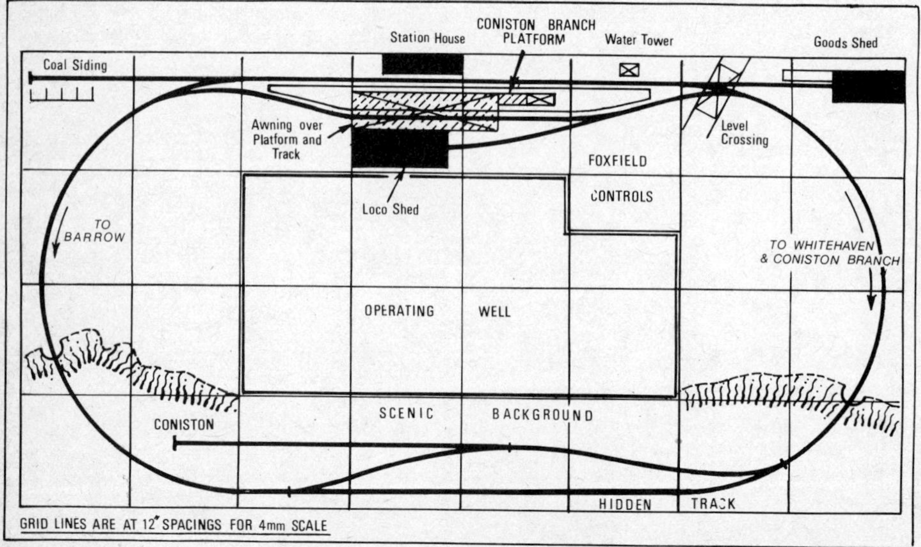